D0184408

17595

14 OCT 1952

THE AUTHORITY OF
THE SCRIPTURES

THE AUTHORITY OF THE SCRIPTURES

BY

J. W. C. WAND

Bishop of London

I go to the Bible—I would bid you go to it—
because I feel how much darkness surrounds you and
me; because I believe that He, in Whom all light
dwells, is ready to meet us there; to reveal Himself
to us; to guide us onward to the perfect day.

F. D. MAURICE

A. R. MOWBRAY & Co. LIMITED
LONDON AND OXFORD

First published in 1949

PRINTED IN GREAT BRITAIN BY
A. R. MOWBRAY & CO. LIMITED, LONDON AND OXFORD
8798

CONTENTS

THE AUTHORITY OF THE SCRIPTURES

CHAPTER I

INTRODUCTORY

THE Church of England uses the Bible in its public services more than any other section of Christendom. The Psalter is read through once a month, the New Testament twice a year, the Old Testament once a year; and a yearly reading is given to the most valuable parts of the Apocrypha. In addition to this there is the regular reading of the Epistles and Gospels at the Eucharist, to say nothing of the psalms and other portions of Scripture in the occasional offices. It is natural, therefore, that Anglicans should be particularly anxious to know what is the nature of this Book to which so much attention is given. How did it come to be written? Whence did it derive its authority? How is it to be interpreted? In what sense is it the Word of God? How ought it to be read? These are some of the questions to which we shall seek an answer in this book.

It should be realized at the outset—and this is an extremely important point—that the Bible is not just one Book. It is, as a matter of fact, a whole library of books. There are eighty of them in all: thirty-nine in the Old Testament, fourteen in the Apocrypha, and twenty-seven in the New Testament. A few are different volumes of the same work, but most are genuinely different works. Each of these separate books presents its own characteristic viewpoint, and varies from most of the other books in the type of literature it represents, in the date at which it was written, and in the special genius of its author. These separate books belong to widely different ages. In the form in which we have them now they cover roughly a thousand years of Hebrew history. In fact, they are a national anthology. The best parallel to the Bible in modern literature would be those series of volumes giving selected extracts from English literature of all the ages, beginning with Cædmon or Chaucer and coming down to Tennyson or Kipling.

But these books were not all written in the same language. The original language of the Old Testament was Hebrew, that of the New Testament, Greek, while some of the books of the Apocrypha were written in one of these two languages and some in the other. Consequently, to be able to read the Scriptures at first-hand, you require a knowledge of two ancient languages, and that a rather specialized one. The Hebrew of the Old Testament is the classical Hebrew and not one of the various modified forms that replaced it later, although it is disputed how far Aramaic was used in some instances. On the other hand, the Greek of the New Testament is not the classical Greek, but a colloquial variety of it that was spoken in Alexandria and other towns of the Levant at the beginning of the Christian era.

A knowledge of the original languages is not, however, necessary to a good understanding of the Bible. For most practical purposes the standard English versions are sufficient. The Authorized Version holds first place as literature, while the Revised Version is able to draw on a better knowledge of the text and a greater understanding of the historical background. Both these versions, however, are so well known and are couched in such a style that they do not always grip our attention as a modern book normally does. It is well, therefore, if the reader takes advantage of some of the more modern versions. The most scholarly is that of Dr. Moffatt, but that strives after such meticulous accuracy that the English style generally suffers, and the scholarship is sometimes too adventurous in seizing upon a fascinating but not thoroughly justified reading. The American Standard Version is good. A much better translation from the point of view of style is *The New Testament in English*, by Mgr. Ronald Knox. An attempt has been made to put the New Testament into 'basic' English, but this is not recommended.

It may have seemed surprising to some readers that the Apocrypha should have been included among the books of the Bible as within the scope of our discussion. A sufficient justification of this inclusion could be found in the fact that the Church of England, in common with other historic Churches, reads selected passages from it in the course of public worship. But apart from this there is good reason for not excluding all consideration of the Apocrypha. As we shall see later, some of its books justify their inclusion on their own merits as religious literature. Historically, too, there is good reason for the inclusion. The two greatest centres of Jewish piety during the last century B.C. were Palestine and Egypt. In each of these the Canon of Sacred Scripture was developed. In Palestine, the home of traditional Judaism, there was a rather strict standard, while in Alexandria among the more liberal Jews of the Dispersion there was greater freedom. The Palestinian Canon did not admit some of the books that were admitted into the Alexandrian Canon. Our Apocrypha represents the difference between the Canons of Palestine and Egypt. As there was from the beginning this measure of doubt as to whether these books should be admitted into the list of Sacred Scriptures, it is perhaps well that our own Church has developed a somewhat cautious attitude with regard to them. It will not admit that the Apocrypha stands on the same level as the rest of the Scriptures, and consequently will not use them as a source-book for Christian doctrine, but it does regard them as valuable for moral instruction. As Article VI says of these books: 'The Church doth read [them] for example of life and instruction of manners; but yet doth it not apply them to establish any doctrine.'

There is extant an Apocrypha of the New Testament as there is of the Old, but the Canon of the New Testament was finally drawn up by common consent of the whole Church, and although some dubious books struggled for a time for a place within the

which they are mentioned, and they were no doubt extensively used by the authors of our present books.

One of the more interesting occupations of modern scholars has been the effort to disentangle some of these early documents from the present books of the Old Testament. It has been discovered that running through the first six books of the Bible there are four documents which have been lettered J, E, D, and P. The first two of them belong to the eighth century B.C., the third to the seventh, and the last to the fifth century. These have all been used and combined in the compilation of the Hexateuch; that is to say, the first five books (the Pentateuch) together with the Book of Joshua.

One of the most important steps in the literary history of the Hebrews must have been the appointment of a royal scribe. It was a natural vanity of kings to wish to have a record kept of their reigns. We know that Eastern monarchs were no exception to the rule, and that some of the Assyrians, for instance, saw to it that their records were chiselled out of the living rock so that they might last for ever. There appear to have been recorders in Israel as early as the Conquest of Canaan, but we do not hear of a royal secretary being appointed until the time of David. That may be the reason why the records appear to be much more carefully kept from his time, but at least it is clear that as soon as professional scribes were employed there would be a great incentive to the keeping of written records.

Actually, however, the historical books that have

been left to us in the Old Testament are not of the
purely chronicle type. They are not just annals. They
do not merely record events, but they seek to say why
certain events happened. They adorn the tale and
point a moral.

The reason for this method of handling history
can be more clearly seen when it is remembered that
these books are reckoned by the Hebrews among the
prophets. What we know as the historical books are
in fact called the Former Prophets. The classification
is significant. The endeavour is made by the use of
this particular expression to show that God deals with
the nation as well as with the individual. Historical
events do not happen by chance, but according to
the set determination of Jehovah. Nor does Jehovah
Himself act capriciously, but in accordance with strict
justice. Righteousness is as much the rule for the
nation as for the private person, and nations which
transgress that rule must inevitably be punished.

This means, of course, that Hebrew history is written
from the prophetic point of view. There were, as we
know, schools or guilds of prophetic teachers in which
this method of interpeting history would be developed.
But the professional prophet was not always able to
rise above the standard of his secular contemporaries.
The high ideals of prophetic teaching were only
maintained by the influence of those great prophetic
leaders whose names stand out in the history of
Judaism, and who together form a galaxy of inspired
teachers unique in the age-long story of religion.
Some of these, such as Elijah and Elisha, are known

to us through the historical books themselves. Others have left us their own writings which have been enshrined for us in the Old Testament and are known in Jewish classification as the Latter Prophets. Their list begins chronologically with Amos and Hosea, and includes those whom we know as the Minor Prophets as well as the greater prophets, such as Isaiah, Jeremiah, and Ezekiel. Their books are essentially collections of sermons, though sometimes they include descriptions of visions and trances through which it was believed that a knowledge of God's will had been conveyed. Together they form a commentary on the political events of several centuries. They reveal the way in which a few devoted men of great insight and religious genius tried to keep the nation true to the path marked out for it by the will of God.

It was not only upon the historical writings that the prophets had so vast an influence. It is now generally believed that the various codes of law were efforts to canalize the results of prophetic teaching. The most conspicuous example is that of Deuteronomy, which embodies in legal form the prophetic teaching given by Jeremiah. But earlier and later codes exhibit the same phenomenon. Thus the Code of the Covenant given in Exodus xx embodies the teaching of Amos and Hosea, while Leviticus enshrines the teaching of Ezekiel, and a still later system, known as the Priestly Code, to be found mostly in Numbers, represents an effort to enforce such teaching as was given after the return of the exile under leaders like Haggai and Zechariah.

It will be seen from what has just been said that the position of the prophets is central in the Old Testament, and that their influence is of paramount importance in the history of Judaism. It was they who were responsible teachers of the people, and it was they who gave the tone to the whole religious development. This does not mean that the nation at any time lived up to the prophetic ideals. The story is one of continued struggle. Even if from time to time the prophetic influence was accepted, and efforts were made to regulate the lives of the people in accordance with it, nevertheless the spirit of their teaching often eluded the effort at codification, and was defeated either by active opposition or listless apathy.

Two of the books belonging to the section of the Prophets require some special comments. They may be regarded either as historical novels or as novels with a purpose. They are the two small Books of Ruth and Jonah. They were written in order to express the views of those Jews who believed strongly in the mission of their nation to the outside world. There were, in regard to this subject, two opposed tendencies in Judaism. The one is represented by such books as Ezra and Nehemiah in which the emphasis lies upon the exclusive character of the nation and its religion. According to this view, too close an association with other nations meant the danger of dilution and corruption. Every effort, therefore, must be made to wall-in Jerusalem, to keep other people from interfering, and even to separate Jews from any foreign women they had married.

The opposite tendency is represented by Ruth and Jonah. The story of Ruth and her devotion to her mother-in-law is well known, and it does not need repetition. Beautiful as the story is, the sting lies in the tail. The book closes with a small genealogical tree which is hardly noticed by the casual reader. 'Boaz begat Obed, and Obed begat Jesse, and Jesse begat David.' The point is that Ruth, the Moabitess, married the Jew Boaz, and was thus the ancestress of the great King David. Thus it was seen that the national hero was himself the descendant of a foreign woman.

The Book of Jonah expresses the same teaching in its more definitely religious aspect. The prophet is ordered by God to declare His will to the people of Nineveh. Rather than have anything to do with the hated city, the prophet takes a ship going in the opposite direction. He is, however, cast out of the ship, swallowed by a great fish, and cast up on the shore of the land to which God had originally directed him. He is thus compelled, in spite of himself, to declare God's message of salvation to the Ninevites. To his chagrin they repent at his preaching and enter upon the way of salvation. The lesson is reinforced when the prophet querulously complains of the destruction of the tree beneath which he had sheltered after his labours. God answered him: 'Thou hast had pity on the gourd, for the which thou hast not laboured, neither madest it grow; which came up in a night, and perished in a night: and should not I have pity on Nineveh, that great city; wherein are more than sixscore thousand persons that cannot discern between their right hand and their left hand; and also much cattle?' It is the most definite missionary lesson in the whole of the Old Testament.

The section of their literature known to the Hebrews as the Writings consists of a miscellaneous collection of various types. Proverbs and Ecclesiastes represent the practical philosophy of the sages or wise men. Proverbs reduces their views on right conduct to easily remembered aphorisms. The despairing note of Ecclesiastes, 'Vanity of vanities, all is vanity,' is rare in the literature of this hardy and robust people. Indeed, it was redressed by a later editor who sought to correct its view of life by inserting some more cheerful statements within the text itself.

The Hebrews were not given to speculation about metaphysical subjects as were the Greeks. In fact, many of the conclusions, such as the existence of God, His unity and goodness, towards which the Greeks struggled by painful degrees, were taken for granted by the Hebrews. Nevertheless, they had their intellectual difficulties, as all thinking men must have, and one of the greatest efforts to resolve a mental conflict is seen in the Book of Job. There the question is, why even the good are put to so much pain and suffering. The various traditional answers to this question are expressed by Job's friends, but Job finds none of them satisfactory, and in the end is silenced only by a vivid sense of the might and majesty of God, and the utter incapacity of a merely finite mind to grasp His ways. Incidentally, however, through the very faithfulness of his effort to justify God, Job has arrived very near to a doctrine of rewards and punishments in a future world. Thus he reached nearer to a belief in immortality than any Hebrew had done since it had been found impossible to maintain the naïve view that existence beyond the grave was a mere ghostly repetition of life on this side of it. The Book of Job is one of the greatest pieces of literature of all time because it succeeds in lifting a temporal question into the realm of eternity. It belongs vividly to its own day, but because it is utterly sincere to the contemporary position, it penetrates to eternal values and thus becomes the possession of humanity through all the ages.

We have already referred to the Book of Psalms as showing within itself a considerable development. It is perhaps best regarded as the hymn-book of the second temple. Like all hymn-books it has been adapted over and over again to meet the needs and express the beliefs of succeeding ages. It is this continuing process of adaptation that makes it extremely difficult to date any particular psalm. The traditional belief was that they belonged to the period of David. Modern criticism has seen behind many of them the historical conditions of the period of the Maccabees. More recently, however, a German scholar startled the learned world by asserting roundly, 'There are no Maccabean psalms.' The reason for his assertion was precisely the evidence of a continual adaptation. Nowadays the effort to date individual psalms has been generally abandoned and has been replaced by an endeavour to understand the character of the psalms. Stress is now laid upon their liturgical use. They are not to be regarded as the rhapsodies of some lonely poet in his solitary meditations, but as liturgical pieces intended to be used by the individual or the congregation at religious worship. Some would be used on occasions of national rejoicings or penitence; some would be used to avert evil from the individual or to express thanks for an individual deliverance. A number of them may well have been used at coronation services in which the reigning monarch was regarded as the representative of God and acquired himself something of a divine character. It is an interesting experiment for the reader to decide for himself under which heading each separate psalm may fall.

Poetry of a different order is to be found in the Song of Songs. This book was believed by Rénan to be a primitive drama. It consists of a collection of frankly erotic poems which express the Hebrews' delight in physical beauty, and blend in one rhythm, so to speak, the aesthetic qualities of the human form and the beauty of nature. It may seem odd that such obviously secular poetry should be found in a religious anthology, but the two spheres were not so easily separable in Hebrew thought as they may seem to ourselves. In any case, there can be little doubt that when the book was included in the Canon of Old Testament Scripture the meaning of these Songs had already been sublimated to apply to the relations between God and the soul, or, at any rate, between the individual and the divine wisdom. When the Christians took them over, the thought was easily transferred to Christ and the Church. It is interesting to note that this is, in fact, the interpretation given to the Songs in the chapter headings of our Authorized Version.

We have thus run over the history of the composition of the Old Testament and given some illustration of the various types of literature of which it is composed. We must now turn to follow the same line of inquiry in regard to the books of the Apocrypha.

CHAPTER III

THE COMPOSITION OF THE APOCRYPHA

AS we have seen, the term Apocrypha implies the excess of the Greek over the Hebrew Canon of the Old Testament. This is only a roughly accurate description since the lists of books in different Greek versions show certain variations. However, the important point to notice is that a difference in authority between this additional literature and the rest was early recognized. There is an interesting passage in 2 Esdras (xiv. 44-45) which brings this out quite clearly, 'In forty days were written fourscore and fourteen books. And it came to pass, when the forty days were fulfilled, that the Most High spake unto me, saying, The first that thou hast written publish openly, and let the worthy and unworthy read it: but keep the seventy last, that thou mayest deliver them to such as be wise among thy people: for in them is the spring of understanding, the fountain of wisdom, and the stream of knowledge.'

The passage shows that the books, later known as apocryphal, were intended for use only by the well instructed. What we now know as the canonical books were for general reading and instruction, but the others were for the limited few. This reminds us that the term Apocrypha was at first used, in a good sense, of books that must be hidden or kept secret from the common people. It suggested that there was an inner core of secret wisdom which was not to be divulged to the multitude. Soon, however, the title began to take on a more sinister meaning. Origen uses it to describe the pseudepigrapha; that is to say, the books written under assumed names. Later in the fourth century the Greek Church drew a distinction between the canonical books and books which, although they were not to be regarded as fully authoritative, were useful for edification. In the Latin Church, Jerome, about A.D. 420, distinguished between canonical books and ecclesiastical books; that is, books which were used by the Church, but were not regarded as canonical. It was to this latter class that Jerome attached the title Apocrypha. Thus Apocrypha came to have the significance of non-canonical.

These non-canonical books were compiled at a time when the scribe was the most influential official in Judaism. It was he who had been responsible for the final collection of the Old Testament Canon, or rather of the three succeeding Canons of the Law, the Prophets, and the Writings. His function, however, was not completely fulfilled when he had produced this threefold Canon. He went on with more original work of his own. It is this fresh material that we find in various forms in the Apocrypha.

As he had most recently been concerned with editing the Writings, it was perhaps natural that he should produce other like works. The most remarkable are to be found in two new examples of wisdom literature which have an honoured place in

the Apocrypha. They follow the pattern set by
Proverbs and Ecclesiastes. The earlier of them is the
book Ecclesiasticus, sometimes known as the Wisdom
of Jesus, the son of Sirach. It belongs to the second
century B.C. and was written by a Palestinian Jew of
the Sadducean school. The other is the Wisdom of
Solomon, which was written by a Jew of Alexandria
(perhaps by Philo, a contemporary of our Lord), and
shows a markedly Pharisaic type of thought. These
two books are of very considerable literary excellence
and they reveal the extent to which Greek philosophy
influenced Judaism before the opening of the New
Testament period.

There was a specially productive stage in the composition of the Apocrypha which may have occurred
soon after the Maccabean crisis when the Hellenistic
Kings of Syria were trying to make the Jews accept
the Greek culture and manner of life. In the height
of the persecution that ensued upon the Jews' refusal,
the prophetic style was developed in the form of
apocalyptic, a type which the Old Testament includes
in the Book of Daniel. The one outstanding example
of this type contained in our present Apocrypha is
the book known in our version as 2 Esdras. More
commonly it was known as 4 Esdras because it was
supposed to continue the series of which our Old
Testament Ezra is the first volume. It deals with the
end of the world, though some parts of it are concerned with the end of Jerusalem and were probably
written after the fall of Jerusalem in A.D. 70.

Other additions to prophetic literature of the more

normal type are Baruch, a book which was supposed to have been written by Jeremiah's secretary, but some parts of which may belong to the period after the fall of Jerusalem; the Epistle of Jeremy which is chapter vi of Baruch in our Apocrypha (it is a tract addressed to the Jews at Babylon against the worship of idols); and the Prayer of Manasses which is attributed to Manasseh, the King of Judea, when he was in prison.

A different type of addition was made to the collection in the way of Haggadah or illustrative stories. Such new stories are Tobit, which is a romance about the period of the captivity, probably written in Egypt, and Judith, which is a piece of nationalist propaganda.

The book Tobit was described by Luther as 'truly beautiful, wholesome, and profitable fiction.' Its purpose is to encourage the observance of the Law, emphasizing especially the duty of almsgiving. It is a manifesto of the Pharisaic school. It achieves its end by telling the story of a pious Jew who with his son, Tobias, and his wife was captive in Nineveh, at first prospering and then falling on evil days. In spite of the taunts of his wife and others he perseveres in his piety and is at last rescued through the agency of Tobias. The latter is led by the angel Raphael to Raguel whose beautiful and pious daughter is suffering from the attentions of an evil spirit. The demon is exorcized, money is forthcoming, Tobias and the lady marry, and virtue is triumphant. It is romance in the spirit of the time with an excellent moral. Its precise date is difficult to fix, but the insistence on the duty of burying the dead suggests the persecution of Antiochus Epiphanes and the Maccabean revolt.

Possibly to the same date (160-140 B.C.), or to the period of the Roman invasion (63 B.C.), belongs the other romance of this kind, the Book of Judith. It also is Pharisaic in origin and was written to encourage faithfulness to the Law in time of persecution. It tells how, when a Jewish fortress was besieged by enemies and was about to be surrendered, a widow renowned for her piety obtains access to the camp of the enemy general and succeeds in assassinating him, thus delivering her people by her steadfast faith and courage.

Certain additions are made in the Apocrypha to the canonical books by way of correction or of intensification. An example of the former is to be found in the additions to Esther. In the canonical Esther the strictly religious interest is very slight and the name of God never appears. This deficiency is amply supplied in the new material. The additions to Daniel, on the other hand, intensify the hero-worship of the canonical Daniel and heighten his reputation for wisdom and judicial insight. Thus the Song of the Three Children emphasizes his hardships; the Story of Susanna discloses his critical acumen; and Bel and the Dragon is sometimes hailed as having made him the first detective in the history of literature.

The remaining books of our Old Testament Apocrypha form a historical section. 1 Esdras (or 3 Esdras, as it is sometimes called) is a free and in some respects legendary revision of Ezra. It was written by an Alexandrian Jew in the second or first century B.C., and is intended to encourage sufferers from persecution, while at the same time strongly stressing the importance of rebuilding the Temple. 1 Maccabees is a marvellous piece of historical writing, compiled at the beginning of the first century B.C. It is our chief authority for the most heroic period of Jewish history. The interest is mainly Sadducean and nationalist. By contrast, interest is weighted in a more definitely religious and even Pharisaic direction in 2 Maccabees, which is less authentic but more moralistic, and bears much the same relation to 1 Maccabees as the Books of Chronicles to the Books of Kings. It is an abridgement of an earlier work by Jason of Cyrene and was written in the second half of the first century B.C. It is addressed mainly to the Egyptian Jews and is intended to cement their unity with their fellows in Palestine by reminding them that they also are the heirs of the glories of the Maccabean age.

Thus in every way the Apocrypha reveals the transition from the Old Testament to the New. Indeed, without some knowledge of the Apocrypha it is quite impossible to understand how that transition took place.

C

CHAPTER IV

THE COMPOSITION OF THE NEW TESTAMENT

OUR account of the composition of the New Testament may begin with the Epistles of St. Paul. Round about A.D. 50 the Apostle to the Gentiles was writing letters to various churches giving instructions about organization, and about the Christian doctrine and way of life. These letters would be read to the congregations during the church services and would consequently take on from the start something of the character of sacred literature. As they were read in the same services as the Jewish Scriptures, they would tend to be regarded as official documents and later as on a similar level of authority. The reverence given to them would suggest the formation of a canon of Christian Scriptures on the same lines as that of the Old Testament. It was, as we shall see, many generations before this process was complete, but it began as soon as the Early Church set itself to ask what writings were worthy to be read in the public services side by side with the books of the Old Testament. The process would be assisted by the view that in the Christian dispensation God had made a new covenant with His people to replace the old covenant made with Israel, and it would be furthered also by the prestige that was gradually accorded to writings associated with the Apostles.

St. Paul was not the only writer of such epistles. St. Peter was responsible for a letter which was addressed to the church of Asia Minor probably at the time of Nero's persecution (A.D. 64-67). The second letter associated with the name of St. Peter belongs to a much later date. To the same period as 1 Peter belongs an open letter to the Hebrews; that is to say, to Christians of the Jewish race. The letters of St. John are a good deal later and may belong to the period of the reign of Domitian, round about A.D. 96.

In the meantime there had appeared several memoirs of the Founder of Christianity. It was inevitable that from the beginning His immediate disciples should cherish their memories of Jesus, and should hand on to their successors, who had not had the privilege of meeting Him in the flesh, all that they could tell of His preaching and His deeds. Originally these stories would be repeated orally. A separate parable with its explanation, or the account of a miracle, or a piece of dialogue between Jesus and His opponents, and above all the dramatic story of His Passion and Crucifixion, would be repeated over and over again in the characteristic Eastern fashion by a teacher and his hearers. These would, indeed, be repeated so often that they would acquire a fixed form and become stereotyped.

A great step forward was taken when a number of these stories in their stereotyped form were written down and joined together to form a continuous narrative. Such were the earliest memoirs of Jesus, and they lie behind our present Gospels. The nearest equivalent to them still remaining is the Gospel of

St. Mark. Parallel with it was a document, now lost, which consisted mostly of teaching material. This source, which is known to scholars as Q, was used together with St. Mark by the authors of our present first and third Gospels. Each of them had at least two other sources peculiar to himself. One was a separate account of the birth and early days of Jesus and the other was private information gathered from sources not definitely identifiable by us.

If the use of previous material by the four evangelists comes as a surprise to any one who has not before asked himself how the Gospels were originally made up, he should consider the implications of St. Luke's own account of the way in which he came to write his Gospel. 'Many have attempted to give us an ordered account of the affairs which have been brought to a predestined completion in our days in accordance with the narratives of eye witnesses who saw everything from the beginning and have since given themselves up to the ministry of the Word. In the same way, I determined first to trace everything accurately from its beginnings, and then to set it forth as an ordered narrative in order that you may have a certain knowledge of those matters about which you have received oral instruction.' This at least suggests that St. Luke had a number of documents before him and that he combined them with his own knowledge, and that he took all possible pains, as a good historian should, to see that his final account was accurate in every detail.

The purpose behind the production of these Gospels

was not merely that the written record should provide documentary evidence against which the development of oral narratives could henceforth be tested, but also to provide authoritative handbooks which could be used by those teachers who were conducting the Christian mission to the Jewish and pagan world. It is almost certain that there were documents of other kinds used for the same purposes which have not come down to us in their entirety, but traces of which can be found in the Epistles and other writings of the New Testament. One such document was a collection of proof texts showing how the prophecies of the Old Testament were fulfilled in the life of Jesus and in the experiences of the primitive Christian Church. It is possible also that there were catechisms which were used in the instruction of candidates for Baptism; at least it is believed that quotations from them can be found in some of the Epistles. To these must be added early forms of a creed, and also liturgical material which might originally have been borrowed from the services of the temple or the synagogue, but which was soon given a Christian interpretation, and to which were added the specific Christian forms made necessary by the development of distinctively Christian worship in the Eucharist.

But to return to the Gospels. We have to consider that the first three Gospels all take very much the same point of view of their subject-matter. For that reason they are called synoptic. It is true, of course, that each of the writers has his own special interests and his own special genius, which give a distinctive character to his work. Thus St. Mark has the fresh outlook and the vivid sense of colour that characterize the journalist. St. Matthew is more the ecclesiastic who is interested in the rites and ceremonies of religious observance. St. Luke, on the other hand, is much more the professional historian, taking pains to make his literary style worthy of his subject-matter. Nevertheless, all three have the same general attitude towards their task and all deal with it in much the same way.

A striking difference is seen in the fourth Gospel. There we have one of the most fascinating pieces of literature that any age has produced, but its precise character is not easy to explain and its special genius eludes the grasp of the commentator. The keynote is struck in the very first verse. It looks at the narrative which is to follow in the light of eternity. 'In the beginning was the Word,' the uttered thought or reason of God, existing from all eternity but at a given date becoming incarnate in Jesus of Nazareth, the embodiment in time of that eternal Word. Everything is done throughout the Gospel to emphasize this two-fold character of the life of Christ, both temporal and eternal. The author is more definite even than the synoptists about the flesh-and-blood reality of Christ, and he can even correct them in some chronological details, but this strong grasp of the temporal character of Christ is used to bring into clearer illumination the spiritual and eternal quality of all that He says and does and is. Much more than the synoptics, the whole book is an effort to interpret the meaning and character of Jesus for every generation.

Who was its author modern scholars are afraid to say. Whether it was the Apostle John or a younger contemporary of the same name is left an open question by conservative scholars; while there are others who would put the Gospel at too late a date for an apostolic authorship to be possible. On the whole, the most recent evidence, including the discovery of very early manuscripts, suggests that the Gospel must have been written before the end of the first century and could therefore conceivably have been composed by the Apostle John if he was a young man at the time of Christ's death.

We are fortunate in having one book which continues the narrative of events after the death of Christ and provides us with the historical background for the greater part of the Epistles. This is the Acts of the Apostles, which is a second volume of St. Luke's narrative and describes the vicissitudes of the Early Church. The story centres upon the two great Apostles, Peter and Paul, but it tells us something of the life of the Church as a whole and helps us to realize how varied was the scene in which these two great leaders played their part.

There remains one book which belongs to a type of literature unknown to our modern libraries. The Apocalypse or Revelation (the two words mean the same thing) belongs to a type of Jewish literature which has become familiar through modern researches. As we have seen, its most conspicuous representative

in the Bible is the Book of Daniel; but there are a
number of Apocalypses in the Jewish literature of the
period between the close of the Old Testament and
the opening of the New, and, as already pointed out,
one of them—2 Esdras—has found a place in the Old
Testament Apocrypha.   These books treat, for the
most part, of visions, although they sometimes describe
historic events under symbolic forms.   They were
probably written in times of danger when it was
necessary to conceal from possible persecutors the
precise meaning of the terms employed.   The use of
the name Babylon for Rome and of the number 666 to
represent Nero are instances of this kind of conceal-
ment which has made the Apocalypses difficult for
later generations to understand.   The main feature of
the books, so far as their teaching is concerned, is that
in such times of human extremity God found His own
opportunity.   Things having become so bad that the
righteous cannot be delivered by human agency, God
vindicates His own justice, puts forth His own arm,
destroys the wicked, and establishes the good.   In
consequence of this pre-possession with the thought
of deliverance the apocalyptic writers are not concerned as the prophets were with a philosophy of
history.   They do not think of God's will as manifesting
itself in a long chain of causation.   They foreshorten
the picture and bring us face to face with eternity.
As in a cinema we see a picture suddenly thrown upon
the flat surface of the screen, so the Apocalyptists throw
their picture of God's judgement across the screen of
eternity erected immediately in front of one's eyes.

It is sometimes thought that the Revelation of St. John the Divine was not written originally in one piece, but that it consists of apocalyptic visions interspersed with some narrative and homiletic material. It is possible that these separate pieces may have been distributed as leaflets by the underground movement during the reign of Nero. They would have the purpose of heartening the people and preserving Christian morale against government persecution. It is suggested that such leaflets may have been collected together, united into a continuous literary form, and then republished at a time when persecution again threatened during the reign of Domitian.

Thus it is seen how varied is the literature of the New Testament. Although it is smaller than the Old Testament it preserves the general character of that book in being an anthology. As such it presents a selection of the most valuable of the writings of those who lived nearest to the time of Christ and had either known Him themselves or had been acquainted with others who had been in touch with Him.

It is obvious that the agency responsible for this compilation was the Church. As the Jewish Church had collected and preserved its own anthology, so the Christian Church first accepted the Old Testament as part of its own Scriptures and then proceeded to collect its own anthology of Christian writings to place beside it, adding a New Testament to the Old.

We must now go on to consider the history of the collection of all these books into a fixed canon until the Bible reached its present form as we know it.

CHAPTER V

THE FORMATION OF THE CANON

THE term Canon in the present context means the collection of authorized Scriptures. What we have to discuss is the process by which our present list of sacred Writings reached the form in which we have it. If we have any naïve idea that the Bible has always had its present form and has come down from the beginning all in one piece, nothing could more easily disabuse us than a brief review of the history of the Canon. We shall find that each part of the Bible—Old Testament, Apocrypha, and New Testament—has its own separate history in this respect. We must therefore pass under review the process by which each of them has come to include the books now comprised within it.

OLD TESTAMENT

Turning to the Old Testament, we find that the three sections of it, known to the Hebrews as the Law, the Prophets, and the Hagiographa, or Writings, represent successive steps in the formation of the Canon. This, of course, has nothing to do with the history of each separate book. The books which were first admitted to the list of authorized Scriptures need not necessarily have been the first to be written. Conversely, some of the earliest documents may have been late in obtaining admission to the Canon. Consequently, we are concerned now with the formation of the list and not with the history of the individual books themselves. Looking at it in this way, we find that the list of authorized Jewish Scriptures consisted first of the Law, then of the Law plus the Prophets, and then of the Law and the Prophets plus the Writings.

The first indication that the Jews were prepared to accept a document as being officially recognized as Scripture binding upon the whole nation is in 621 B.C., when a Law Book was discovered in the Temple and was ordered by King Josiah to be obeyed by the whole people. This Law Book was almost certainly the book we know as Deuteronomy, either in its present or in some earlier form. As we have already seen, this book embodied a legal code based upon the teaching of the prophet Jeremiah. We have also noted that there were subsequent revisions of the Law embodied in other codes. These codes from time to time obtained official recognition, and were finally gathered into what we know as the Pentateuch or first five books of the Bible, a compilation which the Jews regarded as the Law *par excellence*. It was this compilation which formed the first Canon. There can be little doubt that it was this Law, or selections from it, which Ezra read over to the people after the return from exile about 444 B.C. (or, as some say, 397 B.C.), when it caused so much disturbance to the domestic life of those Hebrews who had married foreign wives. An interesting point, which reinforces this view, is that the Pentateuch was the Canon accepted by the Samaritans. It must therefore have become fixed before the separation of the two communities.

Thus ended the first stage in the development of the Jewish Canon. The details of the second stage are hidden in obscurity. We can take it for granted that the sermons of the prophets and some of the historical books compiled under their influence were read in the services in the synagogues, and so began to acquire an importance parallel to that of the books of the Law. At any rate, we are aware that about the beginning of the third century B.C. the Prophets were already coupled with the Law among the accepted Scriptures. Ecclesiasticus xlix. 10 speaks of the twelve prophets, which shows at least that the number of the minor prophetic writings had already been fixed. Again, in 2 Maccabees ii. 13, we are told that Nehemiah, desirous of founding a library, gathered together the books about the kings and prophets and the books of David and letters of kings about sacred gifts. Judas Maccabbeus is said to have imitated him and to have gathered for permanent keeping all those books that had been scattered by reason of the war. This points to an endeavour to preserve sacred books from a wider list than that of the Pentateuch. If we may rely upon the Jewish classification, we can take this list as including the Former Prophets—that is, the Books of Joshua, Judges, Samuel, and Kings—and the Latter Prophets—that is to say, Isaiah, Jeremiah, Ezekiel, and the twelve. Although the authority of 2 Maccabees cannot be trusted very far, it seems natural that after the devastating experiences of the exile the leaders of the nation should set about the foundation of a national library, and this would no doubt lead to the authoritative recognition of the class of literature that came to be known as the Former and the Latter Prophets.

The next stage came in the collection and authorization of the Hagiographa or Writings. If we can follow the doubtful authority of 2 Maccabees, we may suppose that this movement received an impetus unlike that which helped to produce the collection of Prophets. The nationalistic zeal stirred up by the Maccabees in their struggle against Antiochus Epiphanes would result in the effort to preserve everything that was likely to be of value in consolidating the morale of the nation. This led to the acceptance of the collection known as the poetical books—the Psalms, Proverbs, and Job, together with the five rolls (Song of Songs, Ruth, Lamentations, Ecclesiastes, Esther), and the Books of Daniel, Nehemiah, Ezra, and Chronicles. This classification has been somewhat obscured in our Bible because while it is the order of the Hebrew Scriptures, we have preferred to follow the order of the Greek Version.

The effort to preserve and even to extend the sacred books must have been reinforced by the knowledge that the soldiery of Antiochus was bent on destroying the religious literature in order to break down the resistance of the people. 1 Maccabees i. 56-57 tells us that the soldiers 'rent in pieces the books of the Law which they found, and set them on fire. And

wheresoever was found with any a book of the
covenant, . . . the king's sentence delivered him to
death.' It is possible that books of a sacred character
which had not already been included in an earlier
Canon would receive an enhanced value because, not
being authorized, they would not expose the owner
to the same risks.

It is evident, then, that by the latter half of the
second century the collection of a third list of sacred
books was well under way. The gradual recognition
of a third section is suggested by the prologue to
Ecclesiasticus (133 B.C.), 'Whereas many and great
things have been delivered unto us by the Law and
the Prophets, and by the others that have followed in
their steps,' and again, 'The Law, and the Prophets, and
the other books of our fathers,' and still again, 'The Law
itself, and the prophecies, and the rest of the books.'

If this tendency was evident in Palestine, it was also
to be found among the Jews of the dispersion. Indeed,
in Alexandria it went further, and when the Greek
Version of the Old Testament, known as the Septuagint, was made, there was included in it a number of
books that had not been accepted into the Palestinian
collection. As we have seen, it is this over-plus of the
Greek Version over the Hebrew Scriptures that we
now know as the Apocrypha.

The issue between the smaller and the larger Canon
was decided for the Jews of the home country at a
council held at Jamnia about A.D. 100. At that gather-
ing the Rabbis decided that only those books should
be reckoned as forming part of their Canon which were

to be found in the Palestinian list. Thus the formation of the Canon of the Old Testament proceeded by various stages from 621 B.C. to its final completion in A.D. 100.

APOCRYPHA

It may seem odd that we should talk of the Canon of the Apocrypha when the apocryphal books are generally spoken of as extra-canonical, or at the best as deutero-canonical. But just as the books of the Old Testament are a selection from a larger body of writings, so the Apocrypha has a fringe of other works that strove to achieve recognition as sacred Scripture. Thus the Apocrypha is itself a selection. There is a considerable variety of Apocalypses and other books known as Pseudepigrapha, which were composed in the period between the close of the Old Testament and the beginning of the New, and which might at one time have appeared likely to be placed upon the list of sacred literature.

It was in Alexandria among the Greek-speaking Jews of the dispersion that all these books were most commonly read and most highly admired. In that great centre of Hellenistic culture the Old Testament Canon was not regarded as closed. It is true that the first Canon, that of the Law, was closed and was regarded with even greater reverence than in Palestine. To that extent it was the Canon *par excellence*. The second Canon, that of the Prophets, was also the same for the Jews of Alexandria as for those of Palestine, although in the former centre it does not appear to have been placed on so high a level as the Law. But the third Canon, that of the Hagiographa, or Writings, was still quite fluid in Alexandria and there seemed no reason in the nature of things why other writings should not be incorporated in it.

As we have seen, such possible additions offered themselves in several forms. They might be short stories intended to complete the books already found in the Old Testament, such as the Prayer of Manasses, the Song of the Three Holy Children, and the story of Bel and the Dragon, or they might be continuations of the historical books intended to carry the history to a later date like 1 Esdras and 1 and 2 Maccabees, or they might be new works like the Wisdom of Solomon and the Book of Sirach (Ecclesiasticus), or again they might be religious romances like Tobias and Judith. There might even be an Apocalypse or two like the Book of Enoch and 2 Esdras. That such books were in common use we can judge from the fact that they are actually quoted in the New Testament itself.

No doubt it was the compilation of the Greek Version known as the Septuagint (LXX) which assisted these books to take a place beside the sacred writings; and it was no doubt the authoritative character of that translation which helped to exclude those books which did not find a place on its list. The history of the Septuagint is itself obscure. The tradition is that this translation into Greek was made by seventy or seventy-two Elders at the request of Ptolemy Philadelphus in the third century B.C. It is said that the Elders were shut up until they had completed their work, that each one performed the whole task independently, and that when they compared results their several translations were found to be precisely similar without any differences whatsoever. In actual fact, however, the work must have been spread over a considerable period, as can be seen from the differences in language between one section and another.

As we have already seen, the Septuagint contained a longer list of Hagiographa than did the Palestinian Canon. There was considerable controversy among the Jews themselves as to which of the two was to be regarded as authoritative. The difficulty came to a head when the Temple in Jerusalem was destroyed by Titus in A.D. 70. With its sanctuary gone Palestinian Judaism became very much the religion of a book. It was of fundamental importance to know precisely what were the limits of that book. The controversy was settled at the Council of Jamnia somewhere around A.D. 100, when the Palestinian Jews accepted the shorter list as authoritative. The Alexandrians, unmoved by this decision, insisted on retaining their longer list.

The Christian Church accepted the Septuagint and with it the Alexandrian Canon, including the Apocrypha. It is true that there were some misgivings. The leader of the opposition was Jerome, who nevertheless reluctantly included the extra books in his Vulgate Version. Curiously enough the Eastern Church tended to follow his view on the subject, whereas the Western Church disregarded the criticism and preserved the

D

Apocrypha as part of its Bible. At the Reformation it was seen that the Apocrypha contained suggestions that were in line with some of the doctrines attacked by the continental Reformers, such as prayers for the dead and the intercession of the saints. This put the Apocrypha out of favour with the followers of reformed views. Also the Reformers' religion was even more the religion of a book than Palestinian Judaism. It was therefore, above all things, necessary to know which books were 'inspired' and which were not. Since it might be difficult to argue in favour of the certain inspiration of books about which there had been so much doubt, and which had been actually excluded from one form of the Canon, it was natural that the Reformers should endeavour to ignore the Apocrypha altogether. Nevertheless, it was not until 1827 that the practice developed of printing English Bibles without the Apocrypha, and that omission was made without any official authority on the mere determination of the printers.

NEW TESTAMENT

The story of the formation of the New Testament Canon shows the same features as have already appeared in the case of the Old Testament and the Apocrypha; that is to say, there is the same gradual discrimination between various books and a gradual determination to accept some and to exclude others. The major difference is that in the case of the New Testament we are dealing with books composed during a much shorter period. The writing of the Old Testament and apocryphal literature extended over the best part of a thousand years, whereas the majority of the New Testament books were written in a single generation, and even the latest of them cannot have been composed long after the close of the first century A.D.

The reasons that led the Church to accept some books and to reject others were very much the same as in the earlier instances. Just as the Old Testament books were for the most part associated with the names of the great prophets and religious leaders, so the New Testament books were associated with the names of the Apostles. It is true that this qualification might lead an occasional writer to attach some famous name to his manuscript in order to secure acceptance, but then the question of authenticity was carefully examined. Also additional qualifications, such as edification and orthodoxy, were made to apply.

It is not to be supposed that the writers of the accepted books set about their task with the avowed intention of composing material for insertion in a Canon of sacred Scriptures. There was at first no idea of composing a New Testament Canon to stand side by side with the Old. The Christian Church accepted the Jewish Scriptures as its own, and it was only by slow degrees that the thought of a fresh divine library to serve the purposes of the new dispensation, as the Jewish Scriptures had served the purposes of the old, grew to maturity. We have already suggested that one of the reasons that prompted such a development was the practical fact that first the Epistles and then other Christian writings were read in the services side by side with the Old Testament Scriptures. This practice is actually mentioned by one of the early Christian writers, Justin Martyr, who flourished in the middle of the second century. 'On the day called Sunday, all who live in cities or in the country gather to one place, and the memoirs of the Apostles or the writings of the Prophets are read, as long as time permits; then, when the reader has ceased, the president verbally instructs and exhorts to the imitation of these good things' (*Apology* i. 67).

Another influence that led to the formation of the Canon was the need to guard the faith first against fresh claims to inspiration and then against heretical teaching. Of the former an instance can be found in the rise of the Montanists, a body of people who claimed that they were freshly inspired by the Holy Spirit and that His revelation to them superseded the revelation given to the first generation of Christians by Jesus. It was possibly this movement that gave the first incentive to the authorities to form a list of books containing the revelation which the Church was prepared to accept.

An instance of the second kind is to be found in the spread of the Gnostics, a body of heretical teachers who claimed that they had a secret tradition from the Apostles. Their claim had to be met by the assertion that the only acceptable tradition was that given publicly in the accepted writings and guaranteed by the great sees of apostolic foundation. The author who makes this argument most clear is Irenaeus, who, writing towards the end of the second century, affirms that there are four, and four only, authoritative Gospels. He is so certain of this fact that he regards the four Gospels as being of the same order of nature as the four seasons and the four quarters of the earth.

At about the same period as Irenaeus we have direct evidence of the process of the formation of a Canon in what is known as the Muratorian Fragment, which is a mutilated copy of a list of the works accepted as sacred and authoritative by the Church in Rome. It includes all our New Testament books except the first Epistles of Peter and John, the Epistle of James, and the Epistle to the Hebrews. But it is, of course, possible that they were mentioned in the portion of the manuscript that has been lost. What is especially interesting from our point of view is that this document mentions other works which were competing for acceptance. It actually accepts a writing known as the Apocalypse of Peter, decides against the claims of a famous book known as the Shepherd of Hermas, and also excludes as spurious two Epistles allegedly written by St. Paul to the Laodiceans and Alexandrians.

A little earlier in the second century we are made aware of competing interests in an even more vivid fashion. The heretical teacher, Marcion, a Gnostic of a very individualistic type, composed his own Canon, excluding the whole of the Old Testament and accepting from the New only the Gospel of St. Luke and certain Epistles of St. Paul. On the other hand, Tatian, a pupil of Justin Martyr, shows how generally accepted were the four Gospels, because he compiled out of them a sort of harmony, or composite Gospel, fitting the various sections of the four into one comprehensive scheme, which is known as his *Diatessaron*.

It is no part of our purpose to confuse the issue by mentioning a number of other books that for a time were regarded by many as on the same level as our present New Testament writings. Opinion in favour of our present list gradually hardened. In Alexandria both Clement and Origen had doubts about some of the books. The former does not refer to James or 2 Peter. The latter does refer by name to James, although he does not seem to accept its full authority, and implies that the position of Jude was also uncertain. Origen is the first who explicitly regards the writings of the Old and the New Covenant as being on the same level. Both these writers were doubtful about the authorship of the Epistle to the Hebrews, and Dionysius of Alexandria expresses similar doubts about the Apocalypse. This is sufficient to show how much argument there was about some of the books.

As we saw in connection with the Old Testament an occasion of danger and calamity served to quicken the movement for the compilation of a Canon. One of the objects of the Diocletian persecution at the beginning of the fourth century was to destroy the Christian Scriptures. This led Churchmen to distinguish clearly between those writings that were to be reckoned as Scriptures and those that were not. Some Christians tried to escape, at the same time, condemnation by their own company and punishment by the government through the device of handing over books that were often read but were not regarded as being within the Canon.

After the close of that persecution and the granting of peace to the Church we find Eusebius of Caesarea dividing the writings into three classes: those that were acknowledged, those that were disputed, and those that were spurious. The spurious ones included books which are no longer accepted by us. The first class included the four Gospels, Acts, the fourteen Epistles of St. Paul (including Hebrews), 1 Peter, 1 John, and somewhat doubtfully the Apocalypse. His second class (that is, disputed books) he divided into two sections: (a) books generally recognized, among which he included James, 2 Peter, 2 and 3 John, and Jude, and (b) the non-genuine books which consisted of works now no longer recognized as in the Canon, although he seems to have wondered whether the Apocalypse should not have been numbered among them.

The first person to give a list exactly like our own is St. Athanasius. This agrees with the Canon of the Council of Laodicea about 360, which gives the same list and orders that only these canonical books shall be read in the church. This represents the final decision of the Eastern Church. In the West Jerome and Augustine accepted the same classification and their view was reinforced for the West by the third Council of Carthage, 397. Thus before the end of the fourth century the Canon as we now know it became universally authorized throughout the whole Church.

Chapter VI

INSPIRATION

SO far in trying to answer the question, 'What is the Bible?' we have considered only its external aspects, the number and composition of its books, and their gradual selection into a sacred Canon. Now we must try to drive a little below the surface and ask what the Bible is in its inner character.

The immediate answer that leaps to one's mind when the question is put in this way is that the Bible is an 'inspired' book. The New Testament itself recognizes this claim. St. Paul in writing to Timothy (2 *Tim*. iii. 16) says that every Scripture inspired of God is also profitable for teaching. There the reference is obviously to the books of the Old Testament. New Testament writers also make the same claim for their own writings—witness the repeated assertion of inspiration in the Apocalypse of St. John and the denunciation of any one who dared to add to or detract from the book.

It is this inspiration which distinguishes the Bible from secular literature. It is true that the religious literature of other faiths may also claim to be inspired, but in the present chapter we confine our attention to the distinction between the Bible and secular literature. The inquiry is all the more interesting because we have so far treated the Bible as we would any other book; that is to say, we have traced its literary history exactly as we would trace the literary history of any other national anthology. But now we must make it plain why we set the Bible apart from all secular books.

It is true, of course, that we do sometimes speak even of secular literature as inspired, but the term is then used in a secondary sense only. It is a journalistic and not a scientific use of the term. Even such a mode of speech lends a certain distinction to the Bible because it suggests an implicit comparison with the sacred Scriptures. It refers all other books to the Bible as the standard. The highest compliment that can be bestowed upon a book is to say that it is in this respect worthy of comparison with the sacred Scriptures. A book to which this epithet can be applied partakes to some extent of that high and rare quality which by traditional consent fully belongs to the Bible alone. In other words, the inspiration of the Bible is the substance of which the inspiration of Virgil, Shakespeare, and Goethe is the shadow.

This leads us to ask what we mean by inspiration. The question is not an easy one to answer, and many different answers have in point of fact been given. Perhaps our best method of inquiry will be an empirical one. Instead of taking various definitions of inspiration and seeing how far they can be made to fit the books of the Bible, we can ask what impression the Bible makes upon us and see in what respects such an impression differs from that made by all other books. Thus we may arrive at our view of what Biblical inspiration really means.

It will be generally agreed that the impression made upon the reader of the Bible is twofold. On the one hand, he is bound to be struck by the challenging beauty of many phrases that arrest the attention and stick in the memory. At the first reading of them or on the first occasion when they smite vividly upon the consciousness, 'a bolt is shot back somewhere in the breast.' One is aware that for a moment at least one has been in contact with ultimate reality, and very often that impression abides as a lasting treasure of experience. 'The path of the righteous is as the light of dawn, that shineth more and more unto the perfect day.' 'A man of sorrows, and acquainted with grief.' 'The Lord is my shepherd; I shall not want.' 'In My Father's house are many mansions.' 'Come unto Me, all ye that labour and are heavy laden.' 'God so loved the world, that He gave His only begotten Son.' 'In quietness and in confidence shall be your strength.' It would be possible to fill pages with such sayings. Every reader has his own store of them and probably every one, whether he is conscious of their source or not, uses some of them in his writings or even in ordinary conversation.

But more important than the impression made by words or phrases is the impression conveyed by the whole anthology. Its total effect is far greater than that of any individual sayings, greater even than the impression conveyed by any single one of the constituent books, although it is important to notice how much is gained by the effort to separate the various writers from each other and to understand and grasp their individual message. Indeed, the effect of the teaching as a whole is as of a communication from another world. Its morality is exalted above anything that we know in our temporal sphere. Its sense of the supernatural is far stronger than anything to which we are accustomed; its constant reference to eternal standards is something that we find extremely difficult to accomplish even for a few fleeting moments. In short, the total general impression conveyed by the Bible is that of a breath from heaven.

We have, then, in our reading of the Bible two marked characteristics—the impression gained from selected details and the impression of the whole. Where, then, does inspiration lie? Is it in the words or in the total thought? It would probably be true to say that the traditional answer would affirm the first, while our own contemporary answer would be more likely to affirm the second. Personally I feel that there is something of truth and falsehood in both. It is, therefore, worth while subjecting each to a rather more careful examination.

The tendency to find the inspiration of the Bible in its actual words has led to an excessive veneration for each and every word as it stands. Many commentators have insisted that every word is an organ of divine revelation, and that has led to the view that inspiration is equally distributed in every word. Even the less obviously instructive parts such as the genealogical tables and the sartorial regulations have been taken as inspired; the very order of the words and the punctuation have been endowed with special significance; and where there is no obvious lesson to be learnt from the text as it stands, it has been given a mystical explanation quite removed from its apparent intention. There have even been disputes as to whether the inspiration is confined to the original Hebrew or Greek text, or whether it is to be found also in the various versions, and, if so, to which translations it is confined.

All this is really made impossible by the science of textual or lower criticism. Those who practise this particular skill are aware how difficult it is to discover the original text. But if one cannot be sure of the exact original, how can one be sure of the inspiration of each word? If there are several claimants, which one is to be regarded as inspired at the cost of the rest?

It is obvious that we must allow an inequality of importance among the various words and among the various phrases. If all have not the same certitude they cannot all have the same inspiration. Once the belief in the equality of inspiration is broken, we are able to recognize that some passages and even some books are more inspired than others. There is a gradation in inspiration and we need have no hesitation in feeling preference for some passages or some books over others.

This is especially important in any attempt to assess the value of the Apocrypha. If once the rigid view of inspiration, which would assert its equal quality in every part and then go on to confine it to the narrower Canon, is once broken down we can realize that some of the apocryphal books may very well bear comparison with some of our Old Testament books. Wisdom, for instance, might be regarded as at least as well worth Christian reading as Esther or the Song of Songs. Nor need we hesitate to prefer one book to another even within the Canon itself. Luther, in a well-known comparison between St. Paul and St. James, referred to the latter's letter as 'a right strawy Epistle.'

This obviously leaves us with a right to cherish particularly those phrases which seem to us especially beautiful and full of meaning. There are many such passages each with its own distinctive message. Together they express every emotion of the human heart, bringing refreshment to the weary, solace to the suffering, and further gladness to the joyful. In them the beauty of literature is joined with the strength of religion. Noble thoughts are matched with the music of lovely words. They have all the inspiration that we find in the most lovely passages of secular literature, but we treasure them even more highly because in them *cor ad cor loquitur*, heart speaks to heart, and the voice of God is heard within the human soul.

When we come to examine the thought of the Bible as distinct from its literary expression we find a similar difficulty in giving a clear and concise judgement. There have been those who regard the inspiration of the Bible as resting on the truth of its statements. It was once regarded as necessary to an inspired book that it should be free from every kind of error whether of historical fact or scientific statement. But just as the lower criticism made belief in strictly verbal inspiration impossible, so the higher criticism has made belief in this kind of inspiration impossible.[1] The kind of literary examination to which the Scriptures have been subjected has shown that our present books have, in many cases, been compiled from previously existing documents and that some of them give variant accounts of the same events. Formerly, under the old view of inspiration, it was customary to endeavour to find ways of reconciling these double accounts however much they contradicted each other. Now, however, that is unnecessary. We know that the authors who compiled the books of the Old Testament were not always anxious about exact correctness of detail and often put two statements side by side without smoothing out their differences. As soon as this is recognized, it is obvious that inspiration cannot be identified with mere factual accuracy.

In any case, we could have known from the Bible itself that the various authors did not claim for themselves any immunity from common error on the ground of inspiration. Rather were they content to use the ordinary methods open to every investigator when they wished to make certain of their facts. There is, for instance, an almost modern sense of historical values in the New Testament. Thus, as we have seen, St. Luke in the preamble of his Gospel

[1] While the 'lower' or textual criticism seeks to determine the genuine text and meaning of an author, the 'higher' or historical criticism inquires into the date and composition of the Sacred Books and relates them to the environment in which they were produced.

tells us that before he began to write his narrative he took good care to compare other accounts so that he might decide for himself which was the more accurate, and so provide for his readers the best and most veracious account he was capable of producing.

It is obvious, then, that an inspired writer was not free from the processes of ratiocination that characterize all writers. The old view was that an inspired writer was a more or less unconscious instrument in the hands of God, as the plectrum is the unconscious instrument in the hands of the musician who strikes the lyre, or as a typewriter of the author who strikes its keys. This view, however, was more pagan than either Jewish or Christian. The Hebrew prophets did not prophesy in that kind of way. It is true that some of them had an abnormal psychological make-up and were capable of ecstasy, vision, and possibly of clairvoyance. All that can be seen carefully investigated and described in Joyce's book, *The Inspiration of Prophecy*.[1] But such abnormality was by no means necessary. Most of the prophets were noteworthy, not for such peculiarities, but for the clarity of their insight into the events of contemporary history. They could read the signs of the times, and many of their predictions came from their capacity for judging the trend of current affairs. This was especially true of Isaiah and Jeremiah. Others, like Amos and particularly Hosea, were able to see the hand of God in their own experiences, and even to make new estimates of His character from the circumstances of their own

[1] Oxford University Press, 1910.

personal lives. This means that 'Hebrew prophets are the first philosophers of history because they apprehend events as a significant whole, determined and fashioned by the eternal creative principle, which, while transcending them, is ever creative within them.'[1]

From all this we can see that in modern views the onus of inspiration is shifting, so to speak, from the book to the writer. We do not call a writer inspired because he has written an inspired book, but we call a book inspired because it has been written by an inspired writer. There is, however, no mechanical standard by which we can judge the inspiration of the writer. The fulfilment of his predictions might serve as a rough and ready test by which one could judge the genuineness of the prophet, and that test is actually mentioned in the Old Testament (*Deut*. xviii. 21, 22). But Jeremiah at least thought that on one occasion his prediction was not to be fulfilled, although he was quite certain that God had told him to say what, in fact, he had said. Actually the prophecies were fulfilled in many remarkable instances, but the confident prediction was the result of the inspired insight of the prophet rather than of some actual dictation from on high while under a trance.

In any case, we cannot regard factual accuracy as being a necessary proof of inspiration or its absence as being a proof of the lack of inspiration. The sacred writers enjoyed no gift of infallibility. They had received no more than the common education of their time. Their knowledge of science, geography,

[1] Knight, *The Hebrew Prophetic Consciousness*, p. 162.

and history was often imperfect, and we can in our days correct many of their mistakes. There is, in fact, no external guarantee of inspiration. If I may quote Knight again: 'There is certainly no mechanically applicable criterion of the genuineness of true prophecy. . . . The event in which the prophet sees the unfolding of God's purpose is sure of another interpretation by minds which have not the prophetic vision of the divine love and wisdom and all-controlling providence. It is just this blending of outward and inward, of external fact and inner interpretative faith, which goes to constitute the prophetic consciousness that God has been revealed.'

The fact is that the sacred writers can use every kind of event, experience, or literary material as means by which to convey their message. They can use symbolic gesture, the story of their own domestic unhappiness, myths, legends, songs, history, sermons, philosophic inquiry, drama. In all alike they can express the overwhelming certainty of God in action by which they have become possessed. Their inspiration lies in the intensity of their consciousness of God and their ability first to read His ways and then to interpret them to others. It is this that lifts them above all other writers and makes them worthy of the epithet inspired.

We recognize in their inspiration the work of the Holy Spirit. We know that the Spirit works by quickening man's ordinary faculties. Samson owes his physical strength and Bezaleel his artistic genius to this influence of the Spirit. So the sacred writers

E

have their ordinary capacities vitalized by the Spirit's action. Inspiration does not put man's common faculties to sleep while God is left alone to speak, but it quickens these faculties beyond the point of genius.

This sense of inspiration is its own authority. The sacred writers do not often reason and argue as Job does. More commonly they speak with an almost peremptory directness. 'Thus saith the Lord' is a characteristic formula of the prophets; but of the Apostles also it is recognized that, like their Master, they spoke with authority and not with the submissive pedantry of the scribes.

Moreover, their individual authority was reinforced by that of the company to which they belonged. The inspired writer, it has been said, was never a solitary. His inspiration was recognized and guaranteed by his fellows. 'The spirit of the prophets was subject to the prophets.' In the case of the New Testament we have seen that the authority of its writings was guaranteed by that of the Church. Indeed, it has been agreed throughout sixteen centuries of the Church's history that this collection of books should be accepted as authoritative and inspired. They come to us demanding recognition in virtue of their own intrinsic quality of word and thought, and reinforced by the general acceptance of age-old Christian experience.

CHAPTER VII

REVELATION

IT should be clear from what has been said in the previous chapter that inspiration does not act in a vacuum. A person is not inspired and then let loose on the world to talk at large on any subject he desires. Such a notion may attach itself to the journalistic sense of the word, but inspiration in its full and proper sense is always for a purpose, and, indeed, for one purpose only. That purpose is revelation. Inspiration is the means by which men are made the media of revelation. What, then, is revelation?

The meaning of revelation is simply unveiling, the drawing back of a curtain to disclose what lies behind it. In the theological use of the term the object of this disclosure is God. The utterances of prophet and psalmist, the codes of Jewish law-givers, the maxims of sages, the teaching of Christ, the preaching of His Apostles, the memoirs of the evangelists, and the letters of the great missionary leaders, in fact the whole corpus of the inspired writings, have all one object in view, and that is to make clear to men the character of God and His governance of the world. Inspiration, in other words, is simply the instrument of revelation, the means by which God makes Himself known.

It will be immediately recognized how vastly important is this revelation. If God makes Himself known to man, it is the most important subject of knowledge there can be. The act of revelation must be the most important of all miracles; indeed, the miracle of miracles, the fundamental miracle, upon which all others take their stand. It means that there has been a definite invasion of our world of space and time from the eternal, the supernatural sphere. It means that God, having created the world, has refused to leave it in ignorance of Himself, or to its own vague surmising, and has deliberately guided the minds of certain individuals to discern signs of His presence and indications of His ways, and has bidden them repeat what they have learnt for the benefit of His people.

That is precisely the claim the Bible makes. It affirms over and over again that God has uttered certain words and made certain disclosures about Himself. Nay more, it says that when these efforts on God's part were only partially successful in holding the attention of men, who through their stubbornness and pride continually closed their ears to His message, He finally revealed Himself in the Person of His Son. Thus the Incarnation, the central fact of Christianity, is itself dependent upon God's capacity for self-revelation. It is, indeed, the culmination of God's self-disclosure, but it would never have happened if God had not intended to reveal Himself at all. If the charge, 'Thou art a God that hidest Thyself,' had been wholly true, there would have been neither Bible nor Incarnation.

The question has often been asked whether the

Bible and the events recorded in it are the only medium of revelation. Has God left Himself entirely without a witness in every other sphere of existence? The question when put in that form can only receive the answer No. There are certainly many other ways in which God makes Himself known. Nevertheless, the Bible so far exceeds every other source of the knowledge of God that there are many who limit the term 'revelation' to it alone.

For the greater part of Christian history the difficulty was met by speaking of two different kinds of religion, natural and revealed. Natural religion was that which man ought to be able to attain by the use of his ordinary gifts of intelligence and sincerity. In it were included such truths as the existence and unity of God, a life beyond the grave, and the validity of the moral law. Revealed religion, on the other hand, supplied the Biblical addition to this corpus of natural knowledge, the doctrines of the Trinity, the Person of Christ, the Church, and the Sacraments, as well as the specifically Christian code of conduct.

In modern times there has been a reaction against this clear-cut distinction. It was pointed out that all knowledge of God, by whatever medium acquired, must come from God's own self-disclosure and must therefore be a species of revelation. Further, the growing study of other religions made clear a considerable number of approximations to the standpoint of Christianity, so that the distinction did not appear so sharp as once was thought. Moreover, the new methods of Bible study showed that the Scriptures themselves contained many elements that were scarcely distinguishable from parallel teaching in the sacred writings of other religions. The Old Testament, it is true, displays the historical development by which the more primitive stages gave place to higher knowledge, but even so the final result is hardly presented in such a systematized form that it can be viewed clearly as one whole against a confused background of 'natural' religions. As for the later period, it might be said that the one result of permanent value that has emerged from the critical study of the New Testament is the realization that, so far from there being one standard Christian theology from the outset, nearly all the writers had their own individual schemes of the 'way of salvation.'

For a time, therefore, it looked as if the category of particular revelation might be abandoned by theologians, at least by those who were not tied by any obligation to traditional ways of thought. More recently, however, there has been a marked recovery of emphasis upon the distinctiveness of the revelation given in the Bible. It is no longer denied that God has revealed Himself elsewhere, but it is most strongly affirmed that what is given in the Bible as a whole is quite unique and is really beyond comparison with what is given in any other sacred writings or in any other field of experience whatsoever. It is, therefore, becoming customary to draw a distinction not between 'natural' and 'revealed,' but between a 'general' and a 'special' revelation.

General revelation covers the ground formerly

occupied by 'natural religion.' It would include such truths as are taught by religious leaders apart from the Bible, however such truths were reached. It would include also any true insights gained from the study of nature and of history. 'The starry heavens above and the moral law in the heart of man,' have each paid their quota in the past to men's understanding of life and the universe and of the God from Whom both proceed. All this would be reckoned under the head of 'general revelation.' But what is given in the Bible is a 'special revelation.' It shows how God spoke 'at sundry times and in divers manners in time past unto the fathers by the prophets,' and how in the fullness of time He gave a complete disclosure of Himself in His Son. The Bible is thus an authoritative record of revelation as no other book, or library of books, is or can be. And in being thus an authoritative record it is revelation itself—revelation of a most special kind.

When we come to ask what is the content of this revelation we must be quite sure what we ought to look for. The old idea of revealed religion was that it was contained in carefully articulated propositions; in other words, in dogma. But we have already seen that such agreed statements are not to be found in the New Testament. Inspiration did not come to the writers by way of some theoretical idea or philosophical conception. If it had, the result could no doubt have been presented in clear-cut, logical propositions. Rather it came by way of insight into the meaning of certain events about which the writer had to make up his mind so that he could interpret them to his people.

The significant thing is that behind the event he always saw a Person. The revelation lay in the contact between that Person and himself. It was the communication of mind with mind, 'as a man speaketh with his friend,' through the events of daily intercourse. Even in the Old Testament Jehovah is always depicted as a God Who acts. He does not sit, like the ancient classical gods, at ease upon Olympus, but He is always at work and His acts speak louder than words. This characteristic is seen most clearly in the New Testament when at last God speaks through His Son, in Whose life and death and rising again He stands clearly revealed in the terms of human nature—the only terms that we can thoroughly understand. 'The Scriptures,' it has been well said, 'are the manger in which Christ lies.' There we can contemplate Him with worship and adoration, and in knowing Him we learn to know the Father. Revelation is thus the personal self-disclosure of God Himself.

Such a view means that the Old Testament has a claim to be itself a vehicle of revelation in its own right, although without the New it is not complete. It is possible, of course, to isolate the Old Testament, to stop short of the full revelation, and so to misinterpret the whole.

That is the mistake made by the Jews. It is also possible to exaggerate the part played by the Old Testament and to put it on an equality with the New.

That is the mistake made by some of the Reformers, in spite of the warning given by Christ Himself that He came to fulfil the Law and the Prophets and so to show the light in which they were to be read. It must always be remembered that, as St. Augustine said, the New Testament lies hidden in the Old and that the Old lies open in the New. The Old Testament did reveal God authentically as people were prepared to understand Him. As Dr. Sanday used to say, 'There is a Law of Parsimony in revelation, by which it is not allowed to go beyond what each age is able to grasp and understand.' The later revelation subsumes and completes the earlier. This does not mean that we can dispense with the old. The university graduate does not kick down the ladder by which he has been enabled to mount to his present knowledge. What he was taught in the kindergarten still remains valid although he has long surpassed its level. Indeed, it is more than possible that he now fully understands for the first time much that he was taught there. He owes his present knowledge and his capacity for critical judgement and appreciation to the whole of the educational course.

So it is the whole Bible that is the vehicle of God's special revelation. All of it has not the same value, but it shows how God speaks with stammering lips to little children and with exalted eloquence to the mature. But always it is the same God Who speaks, and we can only understand Him fully as we meet Him and learn to know Him in every stage of His self-disclosure.

CHAPTER VIII

HOW TO INTERPRET THE BIBLE

WHAT we have said so far should help us a good
deal when we ask ourselves how we ought to
interpret the Bible. We cannot very well escape the
question, because we are all aware that in point of fact
many different methods of interpretation are employed.
From our earliest years we have heard preachers use
even the plainest narratives to draw moral lessons,
many of which were not very obvious and seemed to
have only the slightest connection with the text. But,
beyond this, we are aware that certain interpretations
of individual passages have been rejected by the common sense of the Church and have been declared
heretical. And we further know of strange aberrations,
such as those which rely on certain Biblical data for
fixing a precise time for the end of the world, and
others which identify the so-called 'Lost Ten Tribes'
with the Red Indians or with the British people, and
use such an identification as a key to the understanding
of the whole. It is therefore important that we should
have some standard of interpretation which will enable
us to learn from the Bible just what God has willed
to reveal and nothing else.

There can, I think, be no doubt that we ought at
least to begin by reading the Bible as we would any
other book. We must try to understand it in its plain

and literal sense so that we can grasp precisely what it is that the various authors are trying to convey. That surely is the right way to read any book and the only way that is fair to the writer. It is, of course, always possible that a great genius, such as a first-rate poet, may convey more than he consciously intends. He may be dealing with a particular situation but so understand and express the truth of it that he opens a door upon the eternal verities. Afterwards his words may be quoted with effect in regard to many other situations than the one immediately present to his consciousness when he was writing. Nevertheless, even in such a case we should naturally wish to grasp the full meaning of his words first in relation to their original context. It is only so that we can guard against the danger of an illegitimate use of his words and, indeed, against downright misinterpretation. So it is with the Bible; a sound understanding of its literal meaning or of its originally intended meaning is the necessary foundation of any proper system of interpretation.

This being granted there are one or two cautions that must be borne in mind if our interpretation of the intended meaning is to be correct.

First, we must remember that we must not start off with the presupposition that the Bible is all of one piece. This is so important a result of modern scientific study that we need not apologize for repeating the warning. We are not dealing with one book but with an anthology covering a thousand years. It must be expected that religion and conduct will be at different levels in various stages of that period, and that the Bible will reflect them all. In particular, the New Testament, in every case of conflict where theology and morals are concerned, supersedes the Old. This should bring considerable relief to those who are inclined to be distressed at what sometimes appears to be the low standard attained by Old Testament worthies.

Secondly, we must be careful to distinguish the type of literature to which each of the sacred writings belongs. All the books are not intended to be treated with the same wooden literalness that one would use in dealing with a scientific treatise or even a work of history. Some, as we have seen, are poetry, and should be interpreted as such. Apocalyptic writers quite deliberately use a highly metaphorical style. Religious romances cut themselves free from the precise trammels of factual history. It is even possible that the compilers of the early chapters of Genesis were deliberately confusing their geography and placing the primordial paradise in the 'land where the rainbow ends.' All this means that we must try to understand the books of the Bible in accordance with the writers' intention, and not according to some preconceived idea of what is proper to the dignity of Holy Writ.

Thirdly, we must remember above all that what we are reading is a set of religious books. Even if it is possible that some, like the Song of Songs, had originally no particularly pious intention, it is nevertheless precisely because they are susceptible of a religious interpretation that they have found a place in the Canon; and they must therefore be read from that point of view. It is especially important to remember this caution during our present scientific age, when so much time and thought have been spent on disentangling the literary history of the Bible that it is possible for a student to read it without ever penetrating to its religious significance at all. Indeed, it is a well-known fact that many candidates for ordination have revolted against the scientific study of the Scriptures altogether because it seemed to have so little relation to their devotional life and practical work. The remedy for this is to remember always that the Bible is the vehicle of divine revelation, and to ask always what God is saying in each separate writing. 'Let God be the subject of every sentence' is sound advice for every Bible reader.

In spite of these necessary precautions it remains true that the plain and simple meaning of the text must be the first and principal aim of all Bible study. To-day it is more easily possible than ever before to arrive at this meaning. The immense researches into the background of the canonical books have made them far easier to place in their historical, social, and religious setting than has ever been possible since the Canon was first formed. We know far more than ever our grandfathers did about the customs and manner of thought of the Semitic peoples and their neighbours, and this increased knowledge has enabled us to see the meaning of many hitherto obscure passages. We are not yet in a position to clear up every difficult point, and there will always be room for further research, but at least we can be devoutly thankful for the great advance made in recent years.

However, there is one reflection that must give us pause. If so much research is necessary to the proper understanding of the Bible, are then its main benefits confined to the scholar? Ought not the value of a religious book to be equally open to the simple and to the unlearned? There is enough sting in these questions to make us realize that there must be some other method of interpretation than that of diligently exploring the literal meaning. This does not mean that it can ever be wrong to strive after a literal accuracy or that we must not pursue that method as far as is possible for us in our individual state of training. Only upon a firm foundation of factual knowledge can any other interpretation be built, and if ever we get away from that foundation all we erect by any other means will be miserably insecure. But granted that foundation, there is at least one other method which has always been recognized by the Church. This is what is sometimes called the moral interpretation.

There is plenty of justification in the Bible itself for this way of reading the Scriptures. St. Paul tells us that every scripture is valuable for instruction, for edification, for training in righteousness (2 *Tim*. iii. 16). In other words, the object of the Bible is not to supply us with scientific or historical knowledge, but to help us in our moral and religious lives. We have already seen that it was from this point of view that the prophets dealt with their historical material. The books written under their influence are intended to show how God deals with nations, and how His law of righteousness is neglected by them at their peril. In much the same way Jesus Himself deals with the Law, interpreting the Ten Commandments so as to bring out their moral and spiritual force, and summing up the whole of them in the double commandment to love God and our neighbour.

The great difficulty about such interpretation in the past has been that so much of the Old Testament seemed to reflect a moral attitude very far from that of Jesus Himself and of Christianity in general. It was not easy to draw a moral lesson from the wholesale destruction inflicted upon the nation's enemies or upon the innocent family of an offender, nor was it possible to draw much spiritual comfort from the so-called imprecatory psalms with their blessing on those who would take the Babylonian children and 'dash them against the stones.' Some could find profit in such passages by interpreting them of the constant warfare between good and evil. If the children in the last reference were people's sins it was possible without a shock to one's finer sensibilities to pray that they might be destroyed. To make such an adjustment, however, was not easy for every one, and there was a considerable relief for devout minds when the new methods of study made it clear that allowance must be made for the gradual education of God's people, and that the exalted morality of the New Testament could not be expected in the Old. Even such a proviso leaves a very considerable effort at adjustment to be made by the worshippers when the psalms are recited in public services; and a later device suggested in the Anglican Church is to leave certain passages out altogether as inappropriate for liturgical use.

Nevertheless, it is clear that with very minor exceptions the moral teaching of the Bible is open to the average reader. If, as he reads, he asks always, 'What does God teach me by this?' he will never fail to receive edification. The moral interpretation of the Bible, if it is secondary in time and subordinate in scientific accuracy to a literal interpretation, may be regarded as primary in spiritual importance.

Under this head it may be worth while to consider a little further the way in which the New Testament writers make use of the Old Testament. There can, of course, be no doubt of their belief in its value and importance. Certainly our Lord corrected its teaching, but He could do so because He regarded it as pointing to Himself, and in that view His followers fully agreed. Consequently, to the Early Church the Old Testament was the most valuable documentary proof of the Messiahship of Jesus. It is, indeed, as we have seen, most probable that one of their earliest books, which we have unfortunately lost, was a collection of proof texts culled from its pages. Something of the way in which Christian teachers would be likely to use such texts may be gathered from the treatment of Old Testament quotations by the New Testament writers.

That it was not always deemed necessary to stick to the literal and original significance of a passage can be seen at once from the quotation, 'Out of Egypt have I called my son.' In the original context Hosea is referring to the early history of the Israelite people and their delivery from bondage in Egypt, while Matthew makes his words apply to the return of the Holy Family from that country after the death of Herod. In what way was the second event a 'fulfil-ment' of the first? Sometimes it looks as if some later happening had called to a writer's mind a form of words that had been used for a quite different happening in the Old Testament. Compare, for in-stance, the two different applications of the words, 'A bone of Him shall not be broken,' or 'They shall look on Him Whom they have pierced.' Sometimes a quotation from some well-known hymn exactly fits a new situation, as in the case of our Lord's bitter cry from the Cross, 'My God, My God, why didst Thou forsake Me?' More important for our present purpose, it is worth noticing how often He uses Old Testament stories to point a moral; for example, Sodom and Gomorrah, Noah and the Ark, Jonah in the fish, David in his hunger, Moses lifting up the serpent in the wilderness, Elijah and the widow during the famine. But most important of all is Jesus' use of the prophecy of the Suffering Servant to explain the inner meaning of His own mission. The influence of those enigmatic verses can hardly be over-estimated. Indeed, it is often suggested that it was through constant meditation upon these prophecies that He Himself arrived at a clear insight into His own true function as Messiah.

In these instances it appears that the moral interpre-

F

tation often merges into something more purely theological. And that works in two ways. First, the whole of the Old Testament with all its historical and religious content is regarded as pointing towards the New until the Messiah is found in Jesus and the Israel of the Old Covenant is replaced by the New Israel of the Christian Church. And secondly, since the whole of the Old Testament foretells the New, every part of the Old has a share in this prophetic work, and even texts which at first might seem to have no obvious reference to later events may be marshalled to that end, if by any turn of phrase or parallelism of content they may seem capable of a secondary reference.

All this may sometimes seem to us a little forced and unnatural, but the glory of the final revelation is so great that it swallows up, so to speak, within its splendour all the lesser lights of that past history which was also a partial revelation of the character of God.

This last consideration may be taken to excuse or to justify a third method of interpretation which was extremely popular in the earlier days of the Church, although it has since fallen into disrepute; namely, the allegorical. This method was not indigenous to Christianity: it was taken over from the Greeks and Latin philosophers, who, when they found it difficult to abstract a decent meaning from the myths and stories about the gods, began to use the narratives as allegories of virtues and vices. The method was adopted by Philo and was strongly developed in the Christian

catechetical school of Alexandria under the impulse of
its great leader Origen.

What is of special interest for our present point of
view is that the method can find some justification
in the Bible itself. The New Testament sometimes
allegorizes the Old. The most conspicuous example
is St. Paul's use of the story of Moses and the rock
from which water was drawn for the thirsty Israelites
in the wilderness. A Rabbinic legend told how the
rock, once struck, rolled after the people in their
wanderings and provided them with a continuous
supply of fresh water. St. Paul uses the original story
and the legend as an allegory of the age-long susten-
ance provided by Christ. 'They drank of that spiritual
Rock that followed them: and that Rock was Christ'
(1 *Cor*. x. 4). Similarly, the cloud that followed the
Israelites and the sea in which they were nearly
drowned are used as allegories of baptism. 'They
were all baptized in the cloud and in the sea.' St. Peter
in the same way uses the story of Noah and the Flood
as an illustration of the way in which the soul is saved
'by water.'

This allegorizing method is very near akin to that
typology which was traditional as part of the Church's
effort to show how the Old Testament foretold the
New. Thus Abraham offering up his son Isaac is a
'type' of God the Father giving His Son to the death
of the Cross for the salvation of the world. Moses
setting up the serpent in the wilderness is also a type
of the crucifixion. The manna is a type of the Holy
Communion. The Sabbath Day is a type of the saints'

rest in heaven. The scapegoat is a type of the sin-bearing Christ. Examples might be multiplied, but they have become so natural a part of our Christian education that they scarcely cause any surprise. Yet it must be admitted that by later writers the method was often pushed to a quite intolerable extreme. When it is alleged that incidents occurred in the earlier period after a certain pattern, *in order that* they might furnish types or allegories of later events, our credulity is often strained too far. When, for instance, the Epistle of Barnabas tells us that Abraham circumcised 318 men because the numerals 18 (IH) stand for the Name Jesus (ΙΗΣΟΥΣ) and the numeral T (300) is shaped like a cross, we are being asked to believe more than probability can bear.

Nevertheless, it is worth noticing that after a period of comparative quiescence the system of typology is once again being tried by certain scholars, particularly in Oxford. Exegesis of New Testament passages is frequently based on the assumption that they have been deliberately written with a reference to some typological passage in the Old. It would be difficult to say that such an assumption can never be correct, but the fact that the commentators can establish little agreement among themselves, and that the same commentator will often change his mind as to the precise nature of the type intended, is sufficient to give us pause before accepting this as a valuable method for modern use.

Probably no great harm is likely to be done by this method of interpretation so long as types and allegories are used merely in the form of literary illustrations. They may, indeed, be quite valuable for homiletic purposes. But it should be obvious that no doctrine or historical thesis may be built upon them. Otherwise the door would be open to every crank or charlatan with an imagination quick enough to seize upon any fortuitous resemblance between a Biblical text and his own favourite nostrum for healing the ills of the world.

The one safe method of Biblical interpretation is the literal. Let us be quite certain what the author means to say: in most cases that will give us all we need. But in other cases if, for instance, we are puzzled as to the reason why a particular book or passage has found its way into Holy Writ we shall find, on investigation, that the compilers of the Bible have themselves found in such writings a secondary meaning which they have felt to be valuable for the edification of the people of God. An example of this has already been found in the use made of the love poems in the Song of Songs. There the primary reference is certainly to human marriage, but the secondary is to the love between God and the soul or between Christ and the Church. It is always possible that God will convey to our own minds secondary meanings of other passages for our edification. When that happens we shall have the courage to accept them as an added gift, secure in the knowledge that having first recognized the original meaning we are doing no hurt to the sacred text.

CHAPTER IX

THE WORD OF GOD

WE have now to ask ourselves in what sense the Bible is, as it is so often said to be, 'the Word of God.' We have already studied its history sufficiently to know that it is not, as the Book of Mormon is alleged to be, a collection of sheets fallen straight from heaven. Nor can it have been, as the Ten Commandments were said to be, engraved by God upon tables of stone. Its component books were written or compiled by individual authors who each had his own particular genius and who was each inspired or guided by the Spirit of God, in ways we have already considered, to express his genius in the written form that has been preserved for us in the anthology chosen and handed down to us by the authority of the Church.

It is also clear that the Word of God has not been delivered to us in short and concise propositions which we can distinguish out of the Scriptures as having a divine character above and beyond the context in which they are set. It is true that we could select some phrases, such as 'God is Love,' that might seem to bear this character, but the modification which even the New Testament applies to such sentences as the Ten Commandments shows how precarious such an exercise of selective judgement is bound to be, and we are forced to recognize that it is never safe to divorce even the finest passages from their context. Therefore the title, Word of God, if it is to be used at all, as we hold it must, applies to the whole Bible and not to mere parts of it, however supreme their value may be. What, then, does it mean?

I should like to enumerate four ways in which the Bible may be taken to be the Word of God.

First, it is the authoritative record of His dealing with man. It tells how God reveals Himself by the way in which He has moulded human history to His purpose of salvation. We learn how He chose out a people for Himself, trained it in His Law, and prepared within it an environment in which His Son might come to accomplish the scheme of redemption, leaving behind an organization by which His saving work could be carried on until at last His kingdom should be established over all existence.

The Word of God is heard both in the events themselves and in the record of them. The record is a very specific interpretation of history. Actually, of course, every historian interprets the events that he narrates; it is his interpretation that distinguishes the record from a mere chronicle. No two historians agree precisely in their interpretation. One may write from the point of view of kings and dynasties, another from the military point of view, another from the political, and yet others from the biographical, social, psychological, or economic. Here in the Bible is history written from the religious point of view. It shows how, through all the ages, God was working

His purpose out. Many other interpretations of the events here described are possible. Secular historians may trace other purposes in the same period, or proclaim their inability to find any purpose at all. It required a revelation to show us that *this* is what it all meant. God speaks to us in making clear the meaning and purpose of history. The Bible is the Word of God explaining to us how in these particular events He was in the world reconciling man to Himself.

Such a view is quite compatible with a recognition that the various parts of the Bible do not all speak with precisely the same voice. Not all the leaders of Israel, for instance, were clear that the mission of their people was to convert the nations. Some adopted the quite different view that in order to maintain their own purity they should keep other nations at arm's length or even destroy them. It is quite a mistake to think that the Old Testament is in all its parts a 'missionary' book. In fact, there was throughout the whole of Hebrew history a sharp conflict between the expansionist and the exclusivist points of view. Indeed, it might be said that the narrower view triumphed in the Old Israel and that the wider view came into its own only with the New Israel. Nevertheless, it is made clear that the latter was the view that was in line with the ultimate divine purpose. Consequently, the Bible as a whole is seen to be the Word of God proclaiming to mankind the historical plan of salvation.

Secondly, the Bible is the Word of God in that He

speaks to us directly through certain inspired individuals, whose speeches and writings it contains.
It has been common in modern times to hold up
the prophets as the special mouthpieces of this
direct utterance in the Old Testament. We need not
doubt that they will always have pride of place, but
a more balanced exegesis has begun to deliver the
Law and the Writings from the temporary disrepute
into which they had fallen. In them also we hear
the Word of God, although perhaps with not quite
the same certainty and clarity.

Any lack of certainty and clarity is not due to the
revelation itself but to the medium through which it
is given. We hold our treasure in earthen vessels, but
the treasure is there. God's normal method is to use
human media even when giving a special disclosure
of Himself, and we are 'frail earthen vessels and things
of no worth.' It is hardly to be expected, therefore,
that even inspired men will reproduce perfectly all
they are given to say. Scripture must be compared
with Scripture so that the authentic word may be
recognized. God will not relieve us of the necessity
to exercise our ordinary human faculties, which He
has bestowed upon us, if we wish to know His voice.
People sometimes imagine that religion, if it is true,
must be simple and easy. Nothing could be further
from the truth. It is to the sin-burdened soul ready
to sink into despair that Christ says, 'My yoke is easy
and My burden is light.' But when we have accepted
His forgiveness we realize that we have been fitted
with His light harness in order that we may the more

gladly and agilely address ourselves to the tasks He has appointed for us.

Among these tasks one of the most important is to use every means to advance in the knowledge of God and His ways. We are, therefore, in honour bound to study His Word as intelligently as we can. If we do bring earnestness and sincerity to that task we shall not shrink from making the necessary comparisons even in the somewhat difficult field of the Old Testament and so we shall learn to distinguish the Word of God as spoken in the Law, the Prophets, and the Writings. The important thing is to remember that in every part there is a word spoken to oneself. The Word of God by the mouth of His prophets is a word to *me*.

Then, thirdly, the Bible is the Word of God because here speaks the Word-made-Flesh. It is not without significance that the term *Logos* may be translated by either 'word' or 'thought.' The Son is the uttered thought or word of the Father, and consequently He is the Father's final, complete, and absolute self-revelation. That is to say, within the limits of space and time. God has, so to speak, translated Himself into human terms and that translation is to be seen in the Son. If, in other words, we want to know what God is like under the conditions of human nature we can see His glory reflected in the face of Jesus Christ. And it is in the New Testament that Christ Himself is made known to us. Above every other reason the Bible is the Word of God because in it God speaks through His Son.

We must be quite clear what it is that Christ reveals. It is not some exquisite ideal of conduct or some undeniable truth about 'the Fatherhood of God and the brotherhood of man.' It is the truth about His Father and Himself, His relation to God and His mission to man. No doubt He does reveal other things, and they are often a comfort and strength to us, but they are comparatively insignificant beside the all-important truth of this teaching about God and His saving work for man. God Who all through history had spoken to us in so many bits and pieces 'hath in these last days spoken by His Son.' That is what makes the Bible so pre-eminently the Word of God. It is the direct application of the eternal Word to one's own soul.

But, fourthly, the Bible is also the Word of God because it contains the charter for His Church. After the Gospels through which Christ speaks we have in the Acts the story of the first tentative efforts of His Apostles to continue His work through the organization He Himself had started. We are shown how it was endued with His Spirit and gathered strength and courage. We see its life being regulated and its ministry extended.

Then in the Epistles we are similarly shown the first tentative efforts to explain and systematize the faith that had been received from Christ and the scheme of salvation that He had taught. Each writer has his own way of developing this theme, and each can easily be distinguished from the others. There is no one clearly defined system of theology in the New

Testament, but the same essential belief is evident in all the different books: one Lord, one faith, one baptism, one God and Father of us all. The fact that the primordial beginnings of a system are also to be found there is an indication that the Church is expected not to leave everything in its life vague, formless, inchoate, but to order all things so as best to meet the needs, practical and intellectual, of God's people.

To crown all we are shown the triumph of the Church in heaven. Nowhere has modern Biblical study enjoyed more fruitful result than in its elucidation of the apocalyptic literature and particularly of the Apocalypse of St. John. We can now understand something of the terror and persecution in which this kind of writing was produced. We can penetrate beneath the disguises that were intended to conceal its teaching from the eyes of possible foes. We can feel the urge to suffering and steadfast martyrdom engendered by a serene and simple faith. And we can look through the open door into the courts of heaven where the triumphant Church praises the King of kings and Lord of lords for the everlasting joy He has brought to all His saints.

It does not do to leave the Church out of the sphere of revelation. By its means we are linked with the period of the Bible and made heirs of all the ages. The New Israel succeeds to the Old, and as God spoke in times past to the Jewish Church, so now, but much more clearly, He speaks to the Church of Christ. 'Hear, then, what the Spirit saith to the churches.' Because it thus speaks to us to-day the Bible is still the Word of God. It records the history of His dealing with men; it contains His direct word given through Law, Prophets, and Writings; it repeats the voice of the Incarnate Word; it contains the charter of His Church. It is, indeed, that Church which has produced these writings, treasured them, and handed them down so carefully preserved for our reading to-day.

CHAPTER X

HOW TO READ THE BIBLE

IF we accept the view of the Bible outlined in the
preceding chapters we shall certainly want to read
it. Quite apart from any question of duty or ecclesiastical obligation, we shall wish to know what God has
said to His people. Also we shall realize that our own
character may to a large extent depend upon such
reading. A man is known by his friends. To put
ourselves regularly in the company of God, His
prophets and evangelists, is bound in due course to
affect our whole attitude towards life. We shall not
only be influenced by the 'climate of opinion' in which
we spend so much of our time, but we shall also be
encouraged by the precept and example of those whom
we meet in the pages of the Bible to maintain the
struggle on behalf of the best and noblest ideals.

Granted our desire to read, the question then arises
how we can read to the best advantage. The answer
is not quite so simple as it may seem, for within the
one general aim of edification we may have different
immediate purposes in our reading and different
methods may suit different aims. We must adapt our
answer to suit each particular need. But before we
do that there is at least one method we can discuss as
altogether unworthy.

If the general attitude we have adopted throughout
this discussion is correct, it is obvious that no method

of reading will be appropriate that does not demand
the exercise of such intelligence as we are able to
bring to the task. The Bible should not be used as
a charm or a fetish that is expected to work by magic.
Yet such a use of it is not uncommon. People will
open the volume at random and regard the verse
nearest to the thumb of the right hand as God's
immediate word to them in a particular crisis. Or
they will let it fall open of its own accord and regard
the verse that first meets their eye as a heaven-inspired
command. No doubt remarkable results are sometimes obtained in this way. Every one will remember
how St. Augustine's conversion was achieved when
his eye lighted upon the passage of the open book,
'Not in rioting and drunkenness.' But the method is
not essentially Christian. It was applied by pagans to
some of their more famous authors, such as Virgil.
Christians ought not to attempt to tie God down to
such a means of expressing His will. We should read
His Scriptures as intelligent people and submit our
mind and heart to the guidance He has given in the
whole of His Word.

If we are thus disposed to read intelligently, there are
three main attitudes of mind in which we may approach
the Bible. The first is the attitude of interest, the second
is that of study, and the third is that of devotion. It
will be useful to deal with each of these in turn.

INTEREST

It should never be forgotten that the Bible is on
any showing a fascinating book. It is, indeed, the

most interesting national anthology that has ever been compiled. This is so not only because of the intrinsic quality of its contents and the genius of its writers, but also because of the place it has occupied in the civilization and culture of many nations over the most fruitful period of the world's history.

Not to know the Bible is to show oneself an un-educated person. Without some knowledge of it we cannot understand the finest European literature. It is woven into the very texture of our thought. The conscious references to it are even more numerous than those to classical mythology, which are often taken to indicate some standard of education, and the unconscious reproductions of its language and teach-ing are so numerous that if they were extracted most of our literary compositions would fall to pieces.

It is obvious that we must find a natural affinity with so much that forms part of the very breath we breathe. If we have been well brought up, the Bible stories will have been familiar to us from our early years, and we should now have the nostalgic interest of fitting our childish memories into a mature world-view. It is not easy to say how the Scriptures would appear to an intelligent person who came to them for the first time, but if one may judge from experiences in the mission-field, one may conclude that they would be of absorbing fascination. How, then, can one best serve this general interest in one's reading?

I should answer that, for this particular purpose, one should read the Bible as one would read any book of general literature; that is to say, easily and rapidly.

It is best to read one of the modern versions, for that will concentrate the attention on the subject-matter rather than upon the language. It is also advisable to read one author through before beginning another. Many individual books can be read each at a sitting. When that is impracticable, the largest possible section should be read at one time. The object of such long and rapid reading is to enable the whole 'message' of each writer to be absorbed separately. It is very necessary to get a clear idea both of the variety of the Biblical anthology and of the distinctive characteristics of each individual writer.

Bishop Taylor Smith used to say that the first time he had ever read right through the Epistle to the Romans in one unbroken effort was when he was lying in hospital with a broken leg, and that it had brought him such a revelation that he had actually prayed that he might break the other if only he might be vouchsafed such another experience. We may regard the good bishop's enthusiasm as a little exaggerated, but we can well understand his delight in a first connected reading of that great Epistle.

It is true that such a rapid reading may not always be sufficient to give a real grasp even of the main purpose of a Biblical writing. Some of the sacred books, especially the prophets, are too obscure for that. What we badly need is a revision of the old chapter headings with their brief analyses of the text which used to be attached to the Authorized Version. If the headings were well written and distributed over paragraphs in the modern manner, they would make

G

the Bible much more easily intelligible. But even without that help it would be well, in order to cultivate a general interest in the Scriptures, to apply from time to time to each individual writing the same cursory method that we bring to our reading of secular literature. It is the main purport rather than isolated texts that one should first aim to know.[1]

STUDY

Many will not be satisfied with so superficial a method of reading. Granted that they have, by this means, acquired a nodding acquaintance with each individual writer and have learnt the main message he wishes to convey, they will have had their appetite whetted for fuller knowledge and will want to know in greater detail what his precise teaching is. They will also want to see that teaching in the light of its historical context. We know well to-day that no Biblical writing was composed in a vacuum. Each of them was addressed to some particular situation, and can be fully understood only in the light of that situation. It is therefore necessary for any one who would acquire a fair knowledge of the Bible to make some study of its historical background as well as of the text itself.

One cannot do without commentaries, and one must remember that Bible studies have advanced so much in the last two generations as to make the old commentaries obsolete. It is a safe rule that, except for

[1] *The Bible Designed to be Read as Literature*, E. S. Bates (Heinemann), comes nearest to meeting this need.

certain great classics, most theological literature more than fifty years old can be disregarded. In choosing commentaries one must look for modern ones.

It is perhaps well at the outset not to be too ambitious and to be content with only a slight introduction to each book and notes that are comparatively short. For this purpose the *New Commentary on Holy Scripture*, published by S.P.C.K. under the editorship of Gore, Goudge, and Guillaume, can be thoroughly recommended. It covers the whole of the Old and New Testaments as well as the Apocrypha, and it not only fulfils the two conditions just mentioned, but it has also a number of special articles of considerable value which will do much to put the reader on the right road to real Biblical study.

Naturally, however, such a volume cannot do more than effect an introduction to the proper task. Luckily a vast range of commentaries caters for nearly every need, and there is no lack of material, however far the reader wishes to carry his researches. Here we are concerned only with modest requirements, and it will be sufficient to mention two series of commentaries which will adequately meet most needs. The first is the Clarendon Bible, published by the Oxford University Press. It is thoroughly up to date and aims on the academic side to fit the mentality of the upper forms at the public schools, but it is also suitable for those whose practical experience of life has gone much further than that of the schoolboy. The other series is that known as the Westminster Commentaries. They are more advanced than the Clarendon, but still do do not demand a knowledge of the original languages. They are written by Anglican scholars and have in view practical as well as academic needs. Naturally they vary in quality but some of them, such as Driver's *Genesis*, Rackham's *Acts*, and Goudge's 1 *Corinthians*, have become quite famous. Messrs. Methuen are the publishers.

Any young reader who intends to pursue a course of Biblical study throughout his life would be well advised, if he can afford it, to get hold of an interleaved Bible or to persuade a bookbinder to interleave one for him. He will then be able to write his own notes culled from the commentaries he reads. These should be very condensed and written with a fine pencil. It will then be easy to add to them or to get rid of them and replace them with something fuller and more accurate as knowledge grows. This is a particularly valuable method for teachers, lay readers, and the clergy. After a number of years, they will have condensed the pith of whole libraries within their own volume of notes.

DEVOTION

For the devotional reading of the Bible no such elaborate apparatus is necessary. Yet it will benefit from a little thought and care. Naturally all reading for general interest or for study is really subsidiary to the devotional reading, and can be made to help it out and to give substance to it. Our more literary studies will have missed their main point if they do

not help us to hear more clearly God's voice speaking
to men in a particular historical situation. From that
point of vantage it should be easy to hear the same
voice speaking to us in our own circumstances. That,
after all, is the precise purpose of the devotional reading
—to make God's voice sound more clearly in our own
experience—but that, of course, will be more likely
to happen if we have first understood what exactly
He was saying to the people to whom the writing was
originally addressed.

The chief difficulty here is that people do not know
where to begin. One suggestion that may be helpful
is that they should join the Bible-reading Fellowship;
an organization that provides its members with an
ordered scheme and a few short notes to make the
scheme intelligible. This organization has been so
successful that its membership is already reaching
gigantic proportions. Another suggestion is that the
reader should follow the Church's own lectionary.
Reference to the introductory pages of the Prayer
Book or to a kalendar purchased from Mowbrays or
S.P.C.K. will inform him what are the Lessons for the
day, and he can read as few or as many of them as he
likes. He will then have the satisfaction of knowing
that he is reading with the Church, and taking his part
in its daily offering of worship.

However, merely to read passages of Scripture, while
it is valuable in keeping us in constant touch with the
heavenly sphere, is not of itself completely sufficient
for the purposes of devotion. Two further suggestions
may be made.

The first is that the most appealing passages should be learnt by heart. It is only by constant repetition that we shall taste their full flavour. In any case, to have a store of such well-loved passages available for use at any time is a priceless possession. Charles Reade makes one of his heroes say that, when as a prison chaplain he made a personal trial of the rigours of solitary confinement, he would have gone mad if he had not been able to solace himself by repeating from memory passages from the great literary masterpieces. How many of us during the long watches of the night have found a similar solace in repeating well-known psalms or other extracts from the Scriptures. Isaiah li, John xiv, and Psalm xxiii must have comforted many a lonely soul lying upon a bed of sickness.

The second suggestion is to use one's reading as a basis of meditation. After finishing your morning prayers think of the passage you read overnight; picture the scene disclosed in it as vividly as possible; make sure what it all meant, and then ask what it may mean to you. Such an exercise enables us to use all the knowledge we have gained by other methods of reading, and brings it all to a head in an effort to hear God speaking to our own soul. If that is not the best end of all Bible reading it is, at least, a very necessary and religious end, and it makes every effort to understand the Bible thoroughly worth while.

Finally, under the head of devotional reading we might add a note on listening to the Scriptures as they are read in the liturgical services of the Church.

The repetition of the psalms might gain in meaning

if we took with us some such small book of introduction to each psalm as that written by Sanday and Emmett and published by the Oxford University Press in 1918 under the title, *The Psalms Explained*. It would be possible to read the introductions to the psalms appointed for the particular occasion while waiting for the service to begin or even while the opening verses are being chanted. We should thus be able to join in the day's worship much more intelligently and devotionally than we sometimes do.

While the Lessons are being read we should, of course, try to rivet our attention on the subject-matter. In many churches short introductory notes are now read which help us to perceive the main point of the Lesson. We might assist the process by trying to decide for ourselves as the reading goes on why this particular passage was chosen for that day's reading, or we could even try to forecast what portion of it the preacher is likely to choose for his text, or we might ask what we would choose ourselves if ours was the duty and privilege of preaching. All this would help us to keep *en rapport* with the service and to prevent our attention from wandering.

Such efforts are perhaps easier when we are listening to the Epistle and Gospel at the Eucharist. For those who can make the necessary adjustments between the Roman and Anglican kalendar there will be a good deal of interest as well as amusement in Mgr. Ronald Knox's *Epistles and Gospels*, published by Burns & Oates in 1946. In this volume he blends in almost equal proportions his ability as a translator, his devo-

tion as a commentator, and his slyness as a humorist.
It is an exhilarating combination, and a sufficient
proof that neither piety nor learning need ever be dull.

Thus, whether in private or in public, it is the
devotional use of the Bible that is most important
and indeed essential. It is when thus read that, as
St. Paul said to his friend Timothy, the Scriptures
are 'able to make thee wise unto salvation.' It is thus
that they are found to be, as George Herbert said,
'the book of books, the store-house and magazine of
life and comfort.' They teach us whence we come and
whither we go.

> Holy Bible, Book divine,
> Precious treasure, thou art mine:
> Mine to teach me whence I came,
> Mine to teach me what I am.

From this method of reading we learn the principle
of conduct, what should be our attitude towards the
world in which we live and towards our fellow men.
We receive encouragement in every effort we make
towards the good, and learn the way of recovery when
we have fallen. In such reading all our sorrows are
assuaged and all our joys enhanced.

> Who can tell the pleasure,
> Who recount the treasure
> By Thy word imparted
> To the simple-hearted?

And all this happens because by this method of
reading we are put in touch with God. 'The Bible
has been beautifully described as the book of which

God is the Hero, and the chief reason for reading the Bible is that we may grow in the knowledge of God. It is true that knowledge *about* God is a very different thing from knowledge *of* God, and the sort of knowledge of God which the Gospel according to St. John says is "life eternal" cannot be gained from any book. It is the "gift of God." But there is perhaps no means of grace that prepares us better for that gift than the prayerful study of Holy Scripture.'[1]

[1] Green, *The Devotional Use of the Bible*, pp. 11–12.

Chapter XI

THE AUTHORITY OF THE SCRIPTURES

WE come finally to the consideration of that aspect of our subject which gives its title to this little book. We want to know what authority the Scriptures have, how far and in what respects they are binding upon our heart and conscience, our mind and will.

It would be well to be clear first of all in what sphere they are to be regarded as authoritative. After what we have said in previous chapters, we shall not expect the Scriptures to say the last word in matters of science, geography, or history. That there is much of value to be learnt from the Bible, even on such subjects, goes without saying, but it is equally undeniable that knowledge in these matters has proceeded very much further than in the days of the Biblical writers. As we have seen when considering the nature of inspiration, we cannot really expect the writers of our sacred books to go much beyond the knowledge of their times in scientific matters. Divine inspiration did not free the writers from the comparative ignorance of their times, nor did it prevent them from making mistakes in such subjects.

There is, however, a quite different story to tell when we come to the sphere of religion. It is there that we may properly expect books which claim inspiration to be truly authoritative. In regard to the nature of God, the Scriptures have spoken with complete and final authority. We have seen that under the guidance of inspiration, the growth of the knowledge of God was gradual. God did not reveal Himself in His fullness at the beginning of the story, but only at the end after His people had been prepared so that they could comprehend the lesson. The final word is spoken by Christ Himself. He was indeed *the* Word, the eternal Logos, the thought or reason of God embodied in human nature. God's word was uttered not only by the lips of Jesus, but by the example of His whole life upon earth; not only by what He said or did, but by what He was and is.

Jesus revealed the Godhead as Agapé or love. It is that revelation which possesses supreme and final authority. Within the Godhead that love is expressed in a relationship which is described as that of Father, Son, and Holy Spirit, and that relationship too is a part of the final revelation. Many scholars and theologians and many councils of the Church have tried to define it, and the Church has come to a decided mind on the subject, a process whose beginnings can be found already within the Bible. 'The Authority of the Scriptures' guarantees the fact of the tri-unity of Father, Son, and Holy Spirit as the expression of this intensely personal relationship and activity of love.

From this it follows that the sphere of religion includes moral conduct as well as belief in God. It must dictate our fundamental attitude to life and to society. The Bible reveals authoritatively that life has meaning and purpose and that it is worth living. The Scriptures do not suggest that all is perfect; they do not burke the problems of pain and sin. They do, however, reveal that we are placed here for a purpose, and that is that we may acquire a character which will enable us to enjoy that infinitude of bliss which God holds in store for His faithful people. Unless we become 'like' God we could not endure eternity in His presence. It is this that gives purpose and meaning to the life that now is. It is a training ground for eternity. Such a revelation enhances the importance of this life, endowing our time between the cradle and the grave with consequences that have their repercussions in eternity. It is this and this alone which gives true dignity and worth to our time upon earth. Thus for the Christian the life of man is anything but 'solitary, poor, nasty, brutish, and short,' as it may well be for the agnostic or atheist. It is endowed with infinite possibilities and is capable of an infinite glory.

But if human life is given an opportunity for acquiring the quality of God-likeness, the revelation of the Scriptures shows us the way by which that may be done; namely, through the exercise of love. In other words, the Scriptures are authoritative not only in the sphere of religion, but also in that of morals. They do not only tell us what God is like, but they tell us what ought to be the guiding principle of our conduct in order that we may become like Him.

We can only hope to be capable of enjoying eternity in the presence of God if we share the character of God. If that character is love, then love must become the keynote of our character also. We are told that when Christ is manifested, we shall be like Him for we shall see Him as He is (1 *St. John* iii. 2). The full revelation of God's character is so overwhelming that those who accept it must be changed by it. They can desire nothing more than that they may become like the Beloved. The power of God is such that it affects a divine alchemy in our personality, until we become such that His love is more and more perfectly expressed in and through us.

Love in this sense is of course to be taken in its full Christian connotation. It has nothing to do with liking or disliking. It is the bending of the whole personality to the service of others. It is the determined effort to bring about the highest good of all with whom we come in contact, whether they be friend or foe. This is the divine revelation and authoritative rule for the Christian life, not an attitude to be adopted capriciously and spasmodically, according to the mood of the moment, but deliberately and of definite purpose under all conditions and in all circumstances.

If then this double region of religion and morality is the sphere in which the authority of the Scriptures is absolute, we may inquire a little more closely whose authority it is. It is only by a somewhat loose metaphor that we can speak of a book or a whole library of books as being 'authoritative.' They may have said the last word on a subject, but on whose authority has that word been said? The answer to this question is somewhat complex. In the first place the authority must obviously be that of the writers. Once we have dismissed a purely mechanical view of inspiration and allowed for the proper play of each author's individual genius, then we must recognize that the authority with which he speaks must be at least in part his own. We cannot undermine that authority by pointing to the lowly character of the sources upon which he draws. What matters fundamentally about any writer is not the stock from which he derives his material, but the use he makes of it. It is in that use that his genius finds expression.

And here we must recognize a distinction between what men are and what they say. In all personal relations the former is much the more important. Even in the case of a lecturer standing before an audience, his own personal character will provide the most important element in his authority. What he actually says may require some modification if it is to be accepted as balanced truth when seen in cold print, and it is possible that, however careful his phraseology, he may never be able to state the full and complete truth even about the minor sub-division of a subject upon which he is an expert. But his character, fully known or dimly perceived, will to some extent redress the balance of his imperfect words and will leave upon the mind of his audience an impression much closer to the truth than they will receive from his words alone.

In respect of the Biblical writers this impression made by the personal character which shines through the incapacity of mere words and the shortcomings of mere translation is of great importance. They have been in personal contact with the Divine, and the impression they have gained they pass on in some measure to us. We have spoken elsewhere of the literary genius of the scriptural authors. Here we must notice the fact that they were great and good men. Goodness is its own authority, and it is their goodness, as well as their ability to assess and present facts, which forms the first element in the authority of the writers and so of the Scriptures.

The second element in the authority of the Scriptures is contributed by the Church. It is quite impossible to drive a wedge between the Bible and the Church, they belong to each other. As Dodd says, 'It is clear that the Scriptures of the New Testament grew up within the life of the Church. Their selection out of a larger body of writings was a function of its growing corporate life, in response to a developing situation. Consequently the Church is prior to the Scriptures of the New Testament. On the other hand, the "Covenant" ("Testament") itself, that act of God which is attested in the Scriptures, is prior to the Church, for without it there is no Church. This mutual relation between Church and New Testament is fundamental.'[1] Or as Brunner puts it even more strongly, 'Without the Church there would be no Bible.'[2]

This testimony from two first-rate scholars, neither of whom is an Anglican, affords welcome evidence of the growing apprehension of the part played by the Church in the production of the Bible. There is indeed and should be no rivalry between them. The Church, whether of the Old or New Covenant, produced the writers and gave us these books, selecting them from

[1] *The Bible To-day*, p. 8.   [2] *Revelation and Reason*, p. 141.

a larger collection and declaring them alone authoritative. The Christian Church accepted the Old Testament Scriptures at the hand of the Jewish Church and added to them the New Testament Scriptures, and used them for the purposes of its mission. Ever since they have been regarded as the foundation documents of the Church. 'The Church to teach and the Bible to prove' is a saying capable of misinterpretation, nevertheless valuable in explaining the actual situation in a way that may be easily grasped by simple minds. That is certainly the way in which the Scriptures were used by the early Christian generation. It was from the Scripture that they proved the Messiahship of Jesus and other doctrines. While the Church must always go back to the Bible for the guarantee of its teaching, it dare not, at least by Anglican standards, teach anything as necessary to salvation which is not contained within the Biblical revelation. There is thus a two-way action and reaction. The Church authorizes the Bible; the Bible vindicates the Church. It is true, therefore, to say that part, at least, of the authority of the Scriptures is derived from the Church which was God's instrument in producing them and at her best and wisest has always striven to keep her voice identical with theirs.

The third and most important element in the authority of the Scriptures is, of course, God Himself. In them God speaks to man. Here He reveals Himself for what He is, dimly no doubt in the early stages, but with an ever-brightening clarity until at last we see the full light of truth in Christ.

In speaking of inspiration we tried to show in what way God moved the hearts of certain men to recognize Him for what He is, to interpret His will revealed in the events of history, and to approach Him in the closest personal communion and fellowship. In speaking of revelation we tried to make clear that whatever may be enshrined in any form of words, the important fact about God's self-disclosure was precisely the knowledge of His character which men were able to gain of Him. The whole Bible in all its various books, written by such different hands and covering so wide an expanse of time, is made a unit precisely by this over-all picture of God which is gained from the one story of His unfolding purpose from cover to cover. It may be that it requires a definite and particular miracle to open the eyes of each individual to this vision, but once he has seen it, he knows beyond further possibility of unbelief that God is behind the Bible, and that it is His form which is revealed within it. It is God's voice that speaks and it is His Word that stands out on each page of the Scriptures.

In addition to all this, it should be said that in the last resort a large part of the authority of the Scriptures must lie in the appeal that they make to our own conscience. Through them God speaks to us and our instinctive response is what carries real conviction. When you strike a note on a musical instrument, it may very well produce vibrations which bring a response from another instrument. So when we read the Bible and are properly tuned to it, God's voice

H

awakes a responsive chord in our own hearts. There is a sense of rightness which is the recognition by our whole personality of the absolute value of what we have read. The novelist, Galsworthy, in his Romanes Lecture at Oxford, explaining the creative activity in the mind of a writer of fiction, described the sense of achievement when character and circumstance exactly fitted. He said that at such a moment 'something clicked' in the mind of the author. The description is perhaps as far as one can go in explaining that sense of conviction which was described by our Lord Himself as the work of the Holy Spirit (*St. John* xvi. 8).

The fact is that authority is a reciprocal relation. It is not truly there until it is recognized. The authority of the Scriptures is only completely effective if it is accepted. We can say that it ought to be accepted. We can give reasons for showing why it should be accepted. But it does not really function unless it is met by the echo of the human soul. The writers may claim authority, the Church may give its witness to the justice of their claim, but we shall not hear the imperative call of God unless our hearts and minds are open to it. When we are ready to listen and to respond, the authority is overwhelming. This is the testimony of millions whose whole lives have been affected by the message of the Bible and who rely upon it day by day to support their continuous communion with God.

We are now in a position, having discussed the sphere in which Biblical authority operates and the source from which it flows, to examine a little more closely its nature. It follows from what has been said in the last paragraph that it is not imperative in the sense in which military authority is imperative. If an officer in the army gives an order, the order must be obeyed at once without question. The whole routine of military drill is intended to produce an explicit obedience to the word of command until it causes the soldier to respond automatically as by a reflex action. But the authority of the Bible does not reduce its readers to automatons, rather it enhances and enriches their personality. As Brunner says, 'Since the Bible describes revelation as the "word" of God, it shows clearly that revelation pre-supposes a receptive spiritual subject.'[1] In other words, we must have faith, and that implies intelligent faith. Faith is not an automatic unreasoning response. In the Bible, as Brunner again points out, faith is connected with the 'heart.' This does not mean reason solely nor emotion solely. It is a synonym for the centre of the personality or the personality as a whole.[2] The authority of the Bible, therefore, is that of a loving parent or teacher who desires to see the utmost possible development of the whole person of the pupil or child.

From this it can be seen that the authority of the Bible is not exclusive in the sense of barring all other approaches to truth. 'The Bible and the Bible only, the religion of Protestants,' is not an exact scientific statement. There have indeed been those who have thought that they could draw everything necessary for life, in its moral, intellectual, and emotional aspects,

---

[1] *Revelation and Reason*, p. 416.   [2] ibid., p. 427.

from the Bible, but their efforts have ended in failure. We have seen nearly twenty centuries of advance since the last page of the Bible was written. Science has plumbed depths whose very existence was unsuspected by the first generation of Christians. Art has expressed itself in many varied forms outside the literary expression of beauty to be found in the Scriptures. Consequently it would be absurd to say that we are required to confine ourselves exclusively to the Scriptures. What we can say is that we are required to adopt no standards that are contrary to those of the Scriptures. If our Lord said, 'I am the Way, the Truth, and the Life,' it implies that all goodness, truth, and beauty must be consonant with His character and teaching. In that sense He is the authoritative and absolute standard. Or to put it in another way, His Spirit is the guide to all truth, goodness, and beauty. The revelation consummated in Him is the clue by which alone we can find our way through the labyrinth of this world.

> I give you the end of a golden string,
>   Only wind it into a ball.
> It will lead you in at Heaven's gate,
>   Built in Jerusalem's wall.

It is this aspect of the matter which I think Karl Barth sometimes seems to miss, although even he appears anxious not to claim too much. 'Even the Church,' he says, 'in holding fast to the sacred character or canonicity of each and every part of the Holy Scripture, only asserts that here within the compass of this Scripture has she at her birth heard Jesus Christ speak; and that here and here only, as far as we know, can Jesus Christ speak to us again.'[1] Against this one might set the quotation from Brunner, 'Does any one seriously contend that in the future, instead of turning to Euclid for geometry, to Galileo for physics, to Lyell for geology, we must turn instead, for everything, to the Holy Scriptures?'[2] The point is surely that Jesus does speak to us again in every discovery of truth, goodness, and beauty, but that we should not recognize it as the voice of Jesus unless we had the clue of revelation in our hand.

Perhaps the clearest indication of the nature of scriptural authority is given in the questions asked of the candidate for the priesthood by the ordaining bishop. 'Are you persuaded that the Holy Scriptures contain sufficiently all doctrine required of necessity for eternal salvation through faith in Jesus Christ? and are you determined, out of the said Scriptures to instruct the people committed to your charge, and to teach nothing, as required of necessity to eternal salvation, but that which you shall be persuaded may be concluded and proved by the Scripture.' Here it is to be noticed that the authority of the Scriptures is held to extend so far as to meet every requirement of a soul in search of salvation. Whatever is necessary for salvation is to be found in the Scriptures and nothing that is not found in the Scriptures can be taught as necessary to salvation. Further it is laid upon the teacher that he shall not lay down anything as necessary to salvation which cannot be 'concluded and

---

[1] *Revelation*, edited by Baillie and Martin, pp. 67–68.
[2] *Revelation and Reason*, p. 378.

proved' by the Scriptures. It is not suggested that there may not be many helpful views and theories nor that there may be many allowable pious opinions, but a clear distinction must be drawn between all these and that body of doctrine which is necessary to the soul if it is to be in a state of spiritual health, and no one must ever be threatened with spiritual death who refuses to accept some teaching which cannot be proved from the Scripture itself.

It is very necessary to remember this careful discrimination because there appears to be an inevitable tendency on the part even of Christian teachers to add their own favourite fancies to the body of doctrine that they teach, and often the timid and unlearned cannot distinguish between what is mere speculation and what is definitely Bible teaching. This tendency is confined to no one period of history and to no one presentation of Christianity. It is, therefore, all the more necessary to remember the precise nature of Biblical authority in order that in accepting it we may accept it to the full.

One further thing ought to be said about the nature of this authority. If on the one hand it does not exclude other methods of approach to truth, and if on the other it does not claim a universal authority in every sphere of thought, it must also be recognized that it is not a compulsive authority. This may seem a strange assertion to make when one recalls the Ten Commandments with their stark injunction, 'Thou shalt not,' but, clear-cut as this imperative is, we find that in the New Testament the negative is replaced by the affirmative and that the Ten Commandments are summed up in the twofold duty of loving God and one's neighbour, which by its very nature must be an appeal to the whole moral nature of the individual rather than a mere categorical imperative.

There is, therefore, in Scripture itself a certain change of emphasis which robs the authority of the notion of compulsion. If we recognize the progressive character in the revelation contained in the Scriptures we must recognize also that the authority of the Scriptures cannot be quite so clear-cut as one might otherwise have thought. The fact is that God does not act or work by compulsive enactments, He appeals to the heart, mind, and conscience. Even the Book of Revelation itself depicts the Saviour as standing at the door of the human heart and pleading for permission to enter. 'Behold, I stand at the door and knock' (Rev. iii. 20). He will not force an entry, He will only enter and make Himself at home with those who open freely and gladly to Him.

The authority of the Scriptures, then, is neither exclusive nor universal nor compulsive. It proceeds by reason and affection. It is limited. It confines itself to the sphere of religion and morals and it is glad to be reinforced by other interests and conclusions affecting the whole personality. It may be suggested that this is a disappointing conclusion, that what one looks for is an 'infallible' authority, a sure guide that will never let one down, but will always answer with complete clarity and directness every question so that there cannot be any possibility of mistake.

It may be said at once that there is no such infallible authority either in the Bible or elsewhere. It is one of the infirmities of human nature that we are for ever looking for some security that will come to us mechanically and save us the expenditure of effort on our own behalf. Every one wants to be safe, and many feel that there must be somewhere some absolute guarantee of safety. But all that is to belittle our nature as human persons. If God treated us like that and gave us some prescriptive authority on which we could always lean without question, we could not possibly grow to the full stature of our own nature. If our life on this earth is a school, a training ground, to enable us to attain that kind of character which alone will qualify us to enjoy the infinitude of bliss that God has prepared for those who love Him, then that character can only be acquired as we are continually making decisions, exercising judgement, surmounting doubts and difficulties, and in every way throwing ourselves on the side of what we believe to be good against all that is evil. For that very reason we must be left to find our way about the seas of life. A chart has been put into our hands, we have to learn to read it and to rely upon our capacity with God's help to steer our course by it.

What, then, is the guide? I suggest that it is threefold. First comes reason or conscience, our God-given instinct for what is good reinforced by such training as we have received. It is, of course, obvious that this instinct does need education. People may sometimes act in a good conscience but in a manner which would be abhorrent to them later when they have been better informed. Granted, however, that we are doing our best to profit by all the illumination we can find, then we may surely take our conscience as a very valuable guide.

Secondly, to the conscience we may add the Church, which we believe, like the conscience itself, to be illuminated by the Holy Spirit. The Church is indeed the very Body of Christ, and the spirit that animates it is the Spirit of Christ. As members of the Church we can accept its teaching, because we believe that it received it originally by revelation from the Son of God and that its formulation of the original testimony has been directed by the Holy Spirit. We need not claim that the Church has never made mistakes, nor should we demand for it that kind of infallibility which we have denied elsewhere; but on the lowest level it could be argued that it is extremely unlikely that the whole Church would make any grievous mistake over any question vital to eternal salvation. The general authority of the Church in teaching and practice reinforces the authority of the individual conscience. The experience of the many may confirm or correct the experience of the one. It may be that sometimes the one may have to recall the many to elements in their own experience which they have forgotten; but normally, at least, the one will find that wisdom lies with the many.

There is less chance of any large-scale error because the Church has the Bible in its hand. There in the foundation documents lies recorded the first fresh impression of contact between God and man. There is the original revelation; and there the truth which brought the Church into being and which she lives to guard stands clear for all to see. There, too, the same voice of the same Spirit speaks as still speaks in Church and conscience, but there it speaks with a plainness and clarity which is all the more important because it reveals the character of a person rather than the carefully articulated formulas of a doctrine. The guidance of conscience, Church, and Bible is the instrument by which the Holy Spirit leads us into all the truth we need.

The Bible thus takes its place as one strand in the threefold cord by which we can secure our hold on the essential realities of life. If it is divorced from the other two, it inevitably loses something of its strength. The Bible is not there to titillate a pseudo-scientific curiosity. It must be read with the full response of the conscience, determining the individual to act on any conviction he may achieve. Nor is the Bible intended as a vade-mecum for an obstinately solitary wayfarer. There is much in it that he will not grasp or understand himself, but he is not intended to be alone, he is meant to be travelling in company with the Church which is always there to advise him. Granted those two prerequisites, how much there is that the Bible does for us. It has a word for us in every sorrow, it redoubles every joy, it offers counsel in every doubt, and it gives warning to every wayward wanderer. It is the instruction of the young, the strength of the mature, the comfort of the aged.

In its mirrors young men can see visions and old men dream dreams. It opens the path of new life to the recovered sinner and brightens the path of every pilgrim to the promised land.

> Lord, Thy Word abideth,
> And our footsteps guideth;
> Who its truth believeth
> Light and joy receiveth.
>
> Word of mercy, giving
> Succour to the living;
> Word of life, supplying
> Comfort to the dying!
>
> O that we discerning
> Its most holy learning,
> Lord, may love and fear Thee,
> Evermore be near Thee.

BOOKS FOR FURTHER READING

(Some have been mentioned in the text)

*The Apocryphal Books of the Old and New Testament.** H. T. Andrews. (Jack) 1908.

The Bible To-day. C. H. Dodd. (C.U.P.) 1946.

The Interpretation of the Bible. C. W. Dugmore. (S.P.C.K.) 1944.

How to Read the Bible. E. J. Goodspeed. (O.U.P.) 1948.

The Devotional Use of the Bible. P. Green. (S.P.C.K.) 1939.

What is the Bible? S. H. Hooke. (S.C.M.) 1948.

The Story of the Bible. F. Kenyon. (Murray) 1936.

Companion to the Bible. T. W. Manson. (T. & T. Clark) 1939.

MORE ADVANCED

*Revelation.** Baillie and Martin. (Faber & Faber) 1937.

The Old Testament, a Reinterpretation. S. A. Cook. (S.P.C.K.) 1936.

*A Fresh Approach to the New Testament.** M. Dibelius. (Nicholson & Watson) 1936.

*The Faith of the New Testament.** A. Nairne. (Longmans) 1920.

Introduction to Books of the Old Testament. Oesterley and Robinson. (S.P.C.K.) 1934.

Revelation and Inspiration in the Old Testament. H. W. Robinson. (O.U.P.) 1946.

The Literary Genius of the New Testament. P. C. Sands. (Clarendon Press) 1932.

Historical Background of the Bible. J. N. Schofield. (Nelson) 1938.

New Testament Idea of Revelation. E. F. Scott. (Scribner) 1935.

DEVOTIONAL

Outline Meditations drawn from the Lessons of the Church. T. W. Crafer. (Faith Press) 1949.

* Out of Print, but probably obtainable at a good library.